Why French Women Feel Young at 50

For a dear friend —

HAPPY BIRTHDAY !

TO MANY MANY MORE ....

love from

Anita

Why French Women Feel Young

at 50 ...and how you can too

Mylène Desclaux

Translated by Alan Thawley

The right of Mylène Desclaux to be identified as the Author of
the Work has been asserted by her in accordance with the
Copyright, Designs and Patents Act 1988.

Originally published as *Les Jeunes Femmes de Cinquante ans*
in France in 2018 by JC Lattès
a division of Hachette Livre

First published in Great Britain in 2018
by HEADLINE HOME
an imprint of HEADLINE PUBLISHING GROUP

1

Cataloguing in Publication Data is available from the British Library

Hardback ISBN 978 1 4722 6185 4
Trade Paperback ISBN 978 1 4722 6187 8
eISBN 978 1 4722 6184 7

Typeset in Bodoni Book by CC Book Production

Printed and bound in Great Britain by Clays Ltd., Elcograf S.p.A.

Headline's policy is to use papers that are natural, renewable and
recyclable products and made from wood grown in sustainable forests.
The logging and manufacturing processes are expected to conform
to the environmental regulations of the country of origin.

HEADLINE PUBLISHING GROUP
An Hachette UK Company
Carmelite House
50 Victoria Embankment
London
EC4Y 0DZ

www.headline.co.uk
www.hachette.co.uk

For Michel

'Age is an abstraction'
My therapist during our last session

(Paris, 7th arrondissement, indecent hourly rate)

Contents

EVERYTHING YOU ALWAYS WANTED TO KNOW ABOUT YOUNG FIFTY-SOMETHINGS 165

The Big 5-0

The day I turned fifty, I was single, my children had left home and I'd stopped working. Two decades earlier, I'd had a baby and set up my own business. I'd been in love and fallen out of love. Then I fell in love again, had another baby and fell back out of love. There were no more children, but in my love life, I carried on more or less following a five-year plan (four men in twenty years).

At that point I was looking for the second chapter of my professional life . . . with no luck. I also wanted to meet someone . . . but no luck there either. And as if a powerful karmic force had brought about a fitting reversal of roles, I was starting to get the brush-off from men on a regular basis. I sensed the workings of natural justice and could hear the amused mutterings of the men I'd left by the wayside. 'Serves you right,' said a voice inside me.

Everything seemed too much: the enforced solitude, the creeping laziness, the weight of the past, the empty nest and the empty bed, the vacuity of the present and above all, the idea that nothing was really going to get any better physically. I realised that with its cult of youth and thirst for the new, society always takes a harsh view of these in-between ages. On the job market or as a potential love interest, fifty-year-old women are not in great demand. There are always people who'll tell you that 'life begins at fifty'. But really? Let's say that between 'it was better before' and 'it's wonderful now', there's a certain moderating truth in the middle.

Am I alone in not feeling defined by my age? And less still by the term 'fifty-something', which makes me think of my mother's generation, when I feel I am so different to those women. I look around me and see that when faced with a choice between wanting their last few rolls of the dice before it's too late and settling down somewhere cosy, today's fifty-year-olds don't hesitate for long. They're brimming with an all-encompassing energy, a kind of agitation that sometimes conceals a feeling of vertigo.

That's something I know a bit about myself, as I'm tightrope walking on a wire. The landscape is sublime, but there's still a chasm under my feet. My balancing bar is threatening to break and send me tumbling down. The personal Jiminy Cricket tucked behind my ear reassures me, whispering that everything's fine, that I'm lucky, that I need to reach for my star. That instead of being afraid of the abyss that's calling to me, I'd be better off immersing myself in the spectacular beauty of this virtual Grand Canyon.

The day I turned fifty, I decided never to talk about my age again, to anyone, and especially not to myself. Clearly, the only way of keeping this promise I hit upon was to start a blog called *HappyQuinqua* [Happy Fifty-Something] and embrace the paradox, whilst considering the advantages of this point in life, which we try our best to think of as mid-life. No, fifty isn't the middle, or three quarters of the way through. It's not the end, or the final part. It's having a clear conscience, standing back from your achievements, it's a sum of experiences, a round figure, and a door opening out on to a street full of things you still haven't explored.

Fifty can be terrible or wonderful. It's certainly easier if we've planned and anticipated, if we've taken the right line into life's hairpin bends. Better if we haven't skidded off course, and better still if we narrowly avoided a wipe out.

We can count ourselves lucky to have been born at a time when fifty gets a little younger every year, thanks to nutrition, improvements in cosmetics and our quality of life. Then if we add in love, humour, a good set of genes and . . . a bit of luck, there you go, ten years younger: a straight flush of perfect conditions.

All the same, in terms of life expectancy – and even though this particular statistic is constantly rising – in my fifties I'm moving further and further away from the mid-point of my life, painfully aware that I've lived through more summers than I have left. Whilst I'm guided by my experiences to an extent, I do my best to keep nostalgia at bay, by making a few compromises with my memories. I eliminate regrets as much as possible, and I do believe that I don't miss any of the hallmarks of my youth: late nights full of energy; feeling fresh the morning after; the irrepressible, impulsive sex; the inappropriate behaviour of the men back then . . . Now, I take pleasure in what's left, and give thanks to be living in an age that provides us with an array of amazing products that were unavailable to our mothers, making our fifties the new forties.

I consciously make an effort to collect amusing, sweet or enjoyable moments, somewhere on the spectrum between *The Small Pleasures of Life* and *The Sweetness of Life**. It's such a pleasure to pluck these nice little anecdotes from everyday life and to share them, never finding life ordinary as it passes by. Recognising the good sides of things: your daily life, your home town, your era, other people, their smiles. Turning situations around to see a brighter side from a different viewpoint, then sprinkling flowers on your words and stars on your heart, with the sole aim of bringing enchantment to the instant. Communicating joy as soon as possible. This is all part of what I've achieved.

And then there are those passive, serene moments that I don't seek out, force or control. Without deciding, emphasising or making a song and dance, I'm finally ready to embrace them. That's probably what happiness is about, according to its simplest etymology: *bonheur* [happiness], *la bonne heure* [the right time]. Perhaps our fifties correspond to this wonderful time that lacks the short, sharp cutting edge of the instant, but is smooth as velvet and has no need to rush. Like a gentle reaction to the acceleration of our lives, I now try to focus a little more on the moment and a little less on the instant.

I wanted to write this book in order to share an objective but benevolent view of women in their fifties –

---

* Translator's note: both were French bestsellers examining the little things that make life worth living.

anecdotal but holistic, caustic but humorous – looking at their transgressions, their courage, their obsessions, their struggles. Women who have to overturn decades of often demeaning prejudices, without ever giving up their daily struggle to stay in the race.

Why French Women Feel Young at 50 is aimed at every woman who suffers that feeling of vertigo caused by the accumulation of years at fifty. Because once we've tamed this acute consciousness of our finite existence, once we've eradicated our complexes about the year of our birth, once we've come to terms with the endemic proliferation of signs of ageing on our necks and the tops of our knees, free at last from the gaze of others upon our bodies, we can finally breathe and continue on our way, at peace and truly in touch with ourselves.

And if along the way, we fancy stopping, pushing back the furniture, turning up the volume and dancing on the table, who can stop us?

No more fifty going on fifteen

One day, in this world of ours that comes up with new classifications to suit the mood of the times, the word *quinquado* appeared, a contraction of *quinquagenaire* [fifty-something] and 'adolescent'. The term, invented by the sociologist Serge Guérin, usually refers to a man or a woman in his or her fifties living the jubilant life of a teenager. An article published in the Swiss newspaper *Le Temps* in 2015 set the ball rolling, followed by a piece in *Le Nouvel Observateur* in France, and so on. They all quoted my blog, presenting me as the archetypal *quinquado*. It was as if they'd suddenly discovered the moon. More and more fifty-somethings of both sexes were enjoying newfound freedom because they were divorced, had no children or because their kids had left home. They had kept in shape by doing sport and had more free time because they were working less (or not at all). So what did they do? What did they buy? Taking the place of housewives under fifty, the favourite target for advertisers and the media, fifty-something *quinquados* were going to be consuming like the thirty-somethings back in the old days.

I remember confidently stating that a *quinquado* was a woman in her fifties who watched her weight, ate seeds, downed seaweed smoothies, seasoned her cooking with yuzu, sprinkled it with chia, did ballet fitness classes, allowed herself dalliances with younger men, scattered the word 'totally' through her sentences and described things as 'awesome'. Which didn't stop her from being a member of a running club, drinking organic beer from the bottle, riding around on a scooter or a bike, playing

Age of Empire online and knowing the names and main characters of all the current must-watch series. Was the phenomenon on the rise, they asked me? Totally!

But soon, the media were painting *quinquados* as women with uncontrollable energy who refused to grow up, went out to nightclubs, borrowed their daughters' ripped jeans, got tattoos on their nether regions, took young lovers (changing them at the drop of a hat) and wore diamonds in their belly buttons. At this point I realised how far removed this sensationalist version was from my idea of a serene evolution. A case in point was a TV report featuring a blonde fifty-something squeezed into a pair of overly tight low-rise jeans going wild on the dancefloor with her daughter before eagerly sticking her tongue down the throat of a young hipster fifteen years her junior. You can just imagine the journalist egging her on: 'Go on, move those hips, we're filming you, and now, give him a kiss . . .'

So let's drop the term *quinquado* and find another way to refer to these women in their fifties, and more than that, women who go through these years taking full responsibility for their lives, in a spirit of curiosity and good humour, focusing all their attention on what does them good.

It's not a question of age. What's new here is the energy they possess and intend to hold on to for as long as possible. These fifty-somethings are into any experience that can enrich their lives. They might go to a rap concert with their kids but also to the opera, go out jogging and walking, read *Elle* and Spinoza, have an older lover and a young husband. Or vice versa.

So call her what you want. For me, she's a woman who's still young, but incidentally also happens to be fifty.

The Question of Age

'The person who continues to hide his age ultimately believes himself to be as young as he would have others believe.'
Jean de La Bruyère, *The Characters*

Should you tell people your age?

Age is both a number and a figure, an addition and a subtraction. It moves, but only in one direction. Age is always going up. We ought to be able to invest in it, like the stock market, for a guaranteed return. Age is a part of us that changes every year. So do we put up with it, or not? How old should we be before we stop telling people

11

our age? It can start very young. Because people who are unhappy with their age will be like that for their whole lives. Those who inflate their age at fifteen will be the same people who subtract some years at fifty. But lying about your age only to have your memory let you down or poring over Photoshop tutorials so you can doctor your passport photo are risky activities, and highly inadvisable.

Lying ages you

One of my good friends systematically takes five years off her age. Whatever the circumstances, without batting an eyelid, she comes out with a number that is not her real age. She can't help it. All of her close friends are in the know but are nice enough to ignore this touch of vanity. Most of the time, it's fine, because she's beautiful and slim and looks ten years younger than she is. After all this time, I suspect she's convinced herself.

I think that when someone has always lied about their age and you find out how old they actually are, it ages them terribly. The lie is counter-productive, and the revelation puts years on you: it makes you seem desperate rather than young. A lie is only effective if it's never found out, and if there's even the slightest possibility of being discovered, you're better off telling the truth from the outset. (Be careful though, this doesn't apply to infidelities: couples can work around a bit of wounded pride, but struggle to recover from knowledge of a betrayal. Best not to have to deal with the complications, which last longer than the initial satisfaction. So keep your nose clean, and everything else for that matter, but that's another story.)

One day, this young fifty-something and her new boyfriend set off for a weekend in Venice. At the airport, they handed over their passports to the border officer, who studied them carefully . . . then handed both documents back to her companion. Glancing at his ladylove's passport, he discovered her date of birth, which obviously didn't match her invented age. Catching his gaze, she realised that he knew. The cat was out of the bag. All of the previous weeks' efforts at concealment cancelled out by an immigration official's blunder. She cursed her lack of attention, she should have stayed focused . . . Her thoughts whirred around her head, eating away at her even on their gondola ride. She tried to forget what was, after all, a minor incident, but it became an obsession. Will he leave me at the end of the weekend because I'm a liar or because I'm too old, she asked herself.

The morning of their departure, she was packing her bags while he was shaving in the bathroom, his passport negligently left on the chest of drawers. So out of pure curiosity – after all, he had seen hers – she opened it. And what a surprise! To her astonishment, happiness or annoyance, she discovered that he had also lied about his age, to the same extent. In their pre-relationship exchange of information, they had both made out they were born five years later. Sharing a lie of the same magnitude is better than a lie on one side, but putting a strain on a budding relationship with this sort of discovery isn't necessarily the best omen for the future. There was no need to take the risk. But ultimately, two people desperate to pass themselves off as younger had found each other.

And besides, at the time of writing, they're still together.

Don't ask . . .

Not asking someone's age is the best way not to be asked your own. When you meet someone, to keep things authentic and on neutral ground, it's better that neither of you knows the other's age. This way, you avoid prejudices and eliminate the feeling of inequality that can be caused by a complex about your number of birthdays, even though you deny its existence. It's a bit like our accent, only less visible.

... *don't tell*

So leave age where it belongs, in the realm of account-ancy, Google data and administrative documents. My experience has taught me that you should never, EVER, tell people your age. We don't give a damn about age, age can f**k off, because the little spark kindled by a look, a few words, a tone of voice or a caress clearly cannot be measured by the information on an ID card, unless the gentleman has designs on procreation – which isn't always the case, especially at the age we're interested in.

Nothing ages you like announcing your age gratu-itously, especially if you're not that young any more. The minute you proclaim how old you are, it sticks to your skin and becomes imprinted on your face as if by magic. Before, you were a person, a voice, a smile, a new possibility, but you suddenly have a label stuck on your forehead, where the horizontal lines that confirm your revelation have now become all too visible. The great thing about something left unsaid, on the other hand, is that it doesn't exist.

Being however old you are is nothing to be particularly proud of. I'm always amazed by the growing number of 'things to be proud of' that people brandish like defensive or even offensive weapons. It's crazy the way people are proud of everything these days. We can be proud of an accomplishment, a success, of graduating or of our children . . . Basically things we've done, achieved or had a hand in. But being proud of your age, your religion or your sexual preferences is a bit strange. These are all intimate details and not up for negotiation.

They just are.

That's it.

The give-aways that you're over fifty

So you've dodged the question, skirted round it with a joke or got out your phone, pretending you've got a text. Basically, you've managed not to reveal your age and glossed over the fact that you didn't answer the question. Well done. But what about all the tell-tale signs? Things it's difficult to hide, or impossible to ignore?

The ages of your brothers, sisters and children

You will have to keep your wits about you to avoid situations that can turn into traps, when certain people (or more likely certain women), without directly asking your age, casually employ a whole battery of tricks that come at the issue from the side, crab-like, which might go something like this:

'Have you got any brothers or sisters?'

'Yes, a brother.'

'How old is he?'

'Fifty-two.'

'So is he older or younger?'

If he's disappointed to discover that you have no brothers or sisters, Mr Curious then turns to the semi-frontal approach that will finally enlighten him:

'Have you got kids?'

'Yes.'

'And how old are they?'

Unless lying comes easy, the answer is enough to blow your cover – bearing in mind, remember, that it's better for people to know you're in your fifties than to find out you're in your fifties and you're a liar. There's a clear advantage here for those who had their kids later in life: the projected effect of their children's ages immediately makes them seem younger, because a young child is the best anti-wrinkle accessory in existence.

But there's also the older child, the one from your previous life. You'd forgotten about him. He's almost thirty, so a couple of questions and answers, and bang goes your instant radiance. Whilst it's relatively easy to hide your age, with the help of a few tricks I've personally put to the test, covering up the existence of your grown-up children is a taller order. And then there are also special cases, earlier marriages, life's little accidents combined with personal or religious convictions. A seventeen-year-old girl could give birth to a daughter who repeats the scenario at the same age as her mother. So the first girl would be a grandmother at thirty-four. And why not a great grandmother twenty years later? Biologically, it's not an aberration, but socially, it's a hard one to live down. Great grandmother at fifty-four! Before long, we'll be able to have children at that age thanks to progress in reproductive science. At which point we'll have to invent some terminology for these new configurations.

In general, politeness dictates that the person who asked the delicately indelicate question about the age of your children shows their surprise with a falsely flattering half-smile. So be prepared for the usual exclamation: 'No!? Incredible!' Or the classic: 'Really? Did you have them very young?'

But once again, be careful. You need to decide if you've been complimented out of politeness, as a pick-up line, or if the person is simply hoping to borrow some money.

Never fall into the trap of coquettishly mentioning your age in the expectation that the other person will be amazed. It's a risky gambit, because through misfortune, malice or lack of sleep, you might fail to inspire the expected reaction. You were fishing for a compliment and receive a slap in the face. A woman who tells you her age for no particular reason is ALWAYS expecting a compliment. And if she doesn't hear the expected 'Really? You don't look it!', be aware that she'll take it as impolite if she's under forty-five, downright rude if she's under fifty-five and a mortal offence if she's any older.

Depending on who asks me the question, I sometimes like to reply: 'Yes, I've got two kids, a four-year-old boy and an eighteen-month-old girl.' A dumbstruck or amused reaction is guaranteed. (As long as no one suggests they can't be mine.) That's my lying fifty-something side, which never comes out for long, but means I can dodge the issue. 'Ha, ha, ha,' we laugh, and move on to something else. Mr Curious or Mrs Devious will struggle to return to the subject without looking as subtle as a bulldozer.

In any case, you can rely on the internet to inform the whole world of your life story and the age you left school, so everyone will realise that if you graduated from a certain school in 1985, you wouldn't have been eight years old at the time. Children and Google are treacherous clues that are hard to escape. Happily (or unhappily), not everyone's interested in you.

So let's take a relaxed approach to the subject, not

hiding behind a mask, embarrassed or compromised. And if some ignorant man or woman should ask you your age to your face in the discreet atmosphere of a shared confidence, remind them with a smile that it's rude to ask and, taking my therapist's example, reply that 'age is an abstraction'. Mind you, I've noticed that it's never someone older who asks the question . . .

Your name

On the chronological scale, your first name betrays at least your generation, if not the year of your birth. If you're a French woman called Geneviève or Jacqueline, you're in your sixties whether you like it or not. If your name is Catherine, Nathalie or Brigitte, you've every chance of being in your fifties. If you're a Caroline or a Stéphanie, you must be in your forties. Answer to Coralie or Astrid? You have to be in your thirties. It's not a rule, just a statistic. Of course, if you're lucky enough to be called Charlotte or Faustine and in your fifties, you have your inspired parents to thank, or your lawyer for taking care of the legal necessities.

Otherwise, you can always try to jazz up your first name by anglicising it: Jane for Jeanne, Ellen for Hélène . . . Or by modernising it: Liane for Éliane, Framboise for

Françoise, Marine for Martine (bad example*), Lily-Rose for Roselyne, Dgini for Geneviève, Mylène for Mireille . . . On the subject of Mylène, I swear it's my real name as stated on my official documents, but only for the past twenty years. My original name has been legally expunged by virtue of my perseverance and thanks to my partner at the time, a lawyer specialising in murders and sects.

No one has ever called me anything but Mylène. On the marvellous day of my birth, my father went to register me at Perpignan town hall, but the clerk decreed that Mylène was not a permissible first name and he had just a few minutes to choose between Marie-Hélène and Marie-Madeleine. My father was already in a state due to the arrival of the first daughter in the family for 120 years, a child who wasn't going to play rugby or belote†. 'You know what? Put what you like!' he replied in his southern accent. My father has always had a reputation for delegating, but he really outdid himself that day. The main point for me here is that I narrowly avoided being called Marie-Madeleine, the kind of name that makes it difficult to get on in life, except in a nunnery.

So that's why I spent over thirty-five years with official

---

* Translator's note: because of its association with the far-right leader Marine Le Pen.

† Translator's note: a popular card game.

documents made out in a name that nobody used. Exam results, flight reservations and official registrations were all situations that filled me with hatred for the arro-gance of that town-hall clerk, or my father's failure to insist upon the name I'd always answered to. Have I ever wanted to go by another name? Never, with the possible exception of the day I finally broke up with a man I'd already spent too much time with (back then, specimens like him weren't yet known as perverse narcissists). As he disappeared from my life for good, he pointed out that Mylène sounded exactly the same as *mille haines* [a thousand hatreds]. It was the most liberating break-up of my life, and one that really was too long in coming . . .

Bumping into people from our former lives

Besides your name, your grown-up children and the lines round your eyes, there are also a whole host of circumstantial clues that show you belong to a different generation to the other people in the room. When an old acquaintance from the distant past makes an unexpected appearance, for example. She recognises you, but you can't place her. Which is always more flattering than the other way around. And you think she looks terribly old, which is not the way you see yourself, but it occurs to you that the ghost from your past might be thinking the same thing about you. No one is happy with the encounter, but the circumstances call for a heartfelt smile from both parties, although the colour drains from my face. Seeing former schoolfriends is depressing: avoid the ordeal! Don't hesitate to turn down invitations to reunions. Nostalgia is terrible for the complexion.

My roots are in the far south of France. I adore my Catalan homeland and my village, which is one of the most beautiful in France. When I'm there, I sometimes bump into certain classmates who are unaffected by urban vanities. These people remember a time when you were 'young but . . .', in other words young, naturally, but with certain defects you wish you'd never had, or at least hope have been forgotten. No, you don't want to be reminded of your fine crop of spots, the barbed-wire braces you used to wear on your teeth, or the glasses that reflected the irony of the world. Since then, you've had Roaccutane for your acne, your teeth have been straightened, and the laser's taken care of your short-sightedness, at least for a while. You imagined your puppy fat was harmoniously distributed but the photos show that your excess weight was mainly located in your cheeks. And let's not even mention those unflattering outfits: whether they were due to a lack of taste or the fashion at the time remains a mystery. And all topped off with some bizarre hairstyles that in retrospect make you shudder with embarrassment. Hairdressers seemed to save their boldest creations for their most bashful young customers.

Then came development, personal fulfilment and satisfaction. Hairdressers now have less power over your style. Time has shaped you; your experience, the people you've met and your children have made you a different person. In a word, you've become you. And then this old friend you haven't seen for thirty-five years plunges you back into the past with an unwelcome remark, suggesting you've lost your accent (oh, so I had an accent, did I?) and adding with an entirely unjustified smile: 'Well, it's just that you talk like you're from the north now!' Grrr, someone needs a slap.

Knowing the words of certain songs

The reason your rendition of 'Chacun fait ce qui lui plaît'* is word-perfect is because you heard it enough times the year you turned twenty to know it by heart for life.

Back then, our brains were like sponges and our memories filed away absolutely everything with no filter.

---

* Translator's note: a huge French hit in the 1980s for the duo Chagrin d'amour, often described as the first French rap track.

And as for belting out songs by Nicolas Peyrac, Joe Dassin or Daniel Balavoine . . . Mostly French songs, because let's face it, we used to sing the English hits more or less without any idea what the words meant!

Your memory

I'd happily swap all the useless details about my neighbours' cousins at summer camp when I was eleven for being able to list all the kings of France or knowing the twenty-five thousand lines of Victor Hugo's *Legend of the Ages* by heart, so I could put on a double act with my brother, who's been serving us up a slice of it at every family meal for forty years. What you learnt at fifteen is set in the marble of your memory, unlike your recent memory, which plays tricks on you every day.

Until I turned forty, I was known for my world-class recall. Then I gradually started forgetting a name here, another there, then a word, then a hundred, then a fact, and then a whole avalanche of misplaced information, including the film that you only remember you've already seen after the first quarter of an hour. 'Uh-oh, must be Alzheimer's!' we laughingly proclaim, knowing that in our heart of hearts, these early signs of old age don't seem that funny.

Not speaking English

It's the great French complex: the over-fifties don't speak English and will never speak it well. That's the way it is. Look at the country's élite, our government ministers and former presidents. It's shameful. 'Sorry for the bad time!'* The few who do speak English well had parents who lived abroad, came from a wealthy urban background and were sufficiently educated to want to send their children to American summer camps or English language colleges for the holidays.

In the 1970s, growing up in the distant provinces, we'd never heard English spoken until our first year of secondary school, and then just for three hours a week. That was it. The internet didn't exist, and films were all dubbed into French. Happily, things are changing, and our children are exposed to English from a very early age, thanks to YouTube and Netflix. But for us, giving up is the only dignified option. Learning English at fifty, forget it! You might just master it and more or less get by through perseverance. But taking part

---

* Translator's note: the words for 'time' and 'weather' are the same in French, and this famously caught Nicolas Sarkozy out during a visit from Hillary Clinton.

in a fluent conversation, expressing yourself quickly, laughing at the right moment or getting through a meal all the way to dessert and following everything that's being said: never.

Today I can read, speak and understand English fairly well, at least for someone of my generation. But in spite of my university studies, numerous lengthy stays in the US over the past few years and workshops at NYU, basically my stubborn desire to make progress, I'm always exhausted after two hours of conversation in English. This immense weariness, which must come from my inner ear, generally overcomes me just before the cheese course. So I give up, or panic and seek out a French-speaking branch to cling to. I can check my level of concentration on a given day with American box sets. Generally, I start out without subtitles, then turn them on in English along the way, and finally, for the next episode, I opt for subtitles in French.

Reading glasses

With the exception of sunglasses, which cover up tired-ness and mean you don't have to say hello to someone you'd rather avoid, and for those under thirty, glasses aren't a good look for anyone, far from it. Only the short-sighted who had laser surgery before the inevitable arrival of long-sightedness can savour putting off the moment when glasses become a necessity.

For a first date, here's a tip: rather than getting out your glasses in the restaurant to read the menu, use the torch function on your phone or simply order the dish of the day. After that, who cares? Love is blind.

Being hopeless with computers

How old were we when we got our first email address? It seems incredible, now that children have mobile phones when they start school at six and an Instagram account the year after. We know nothing about the Cloud and the web. Being out of the loop like this means we're not in control, and unless someone proves otherwise, I can assure you that no one over fifty-five, even if they are internet savvy, knows what TXT or DNS mean. It's like English, we can make progress, but we'll never really speak the language.

Keeping photo albums

Once upon a time, our life stories were told through pictures stuck in an album. At various points – moving house or the end of an uneventful evening – we would get out the boxes of photo albums and flick through the pages, commenting on the events and people's waistlines. Our life stories were illustrated with snapshots of good times and younger-looking people. The box of nostalgia brought back waves of emotions and, with lumps in our throats, we'd put the album back until the next house move or uneventful evening ... Now Apple and the Cloud take care of everything. Images are stored in a dust-free virtual space. And we never look at them.

Holding a big birthday celebration

On top of everything else, should we throw a party to celebrate this extra year, which in itself can inspire depression or murder?

Yes and no.

Yes, because it's always good to have a party. It keeps you young, even if you're clapped out by midnight. Yes, to prove that we don't care and truly believe that age is an abstraction.

No, because someone will always ask the right person how old we are, and in ten years' time, they'll remember the figure and add ten to it. Of course, some people will say: 'Oh, go on! Let's have a party!' Well, no, let's keep quiet. Over fifty, where's the advantage in broadcasting this numerical progression? We can still ignore it, at least for a few years. Then much later, when our vanity has faded, and our friendships have been whittled down to the essential, we can let others take care of it: children, grandchildren, the inner circle.

However, there's nothing to stop you celebrating 'the event' without giving a reason. An elegant solution that will suit all your friends, who won't have to cough up for a present. 'Oh, it was your birthday, you should have said . . .!'

But if you don't throw a party, I hear you say, how do you mark the event and not spend the evening alone brooding and stroking your cat? Don't panic, if there's no tropical sunset or a loving companion in the picture, a bottle from the back of the fridge will do the trick, opened in the kitchen and shared with two or three friends. Light some candles, turn on the stereo, pop a cork and post the pictures straight to Instagram and Facebook, whilst collectively thanking the forty friends who've competed to come up with a wittier, less mundane alternative to the expression 'happy birthday'.

And above all, don't forget that age only becomes a reality when it's compared. For age to be an issue, there have to be older and younger people around you. If no one knows anyone's age, you're all just human beings.

A new way to mark time

The time has come to launch an international appeal for the introduction of a different chronological numbering system to the one we've inherited from the Gregorian calendar. Our system of marking out time is obsolete, dating back to a papal bull published by a Young Pope, Gregory XIII, who didn't imagine for a single second that the quantification of years would create so much discussion. Without him, this book wouldn't exist.

Let's imagine that in the future, programmers got rid of this Excel conception of time and replaced it with something new – why not a digital structure with data stored in a 'cloud', something discreet and virtual? For humans in general (and women in particular), replacing a papal system with a digital one would mean they were born into a relationship to time not defined by a figure, but by a more poetic, less mathematical yardstick, a lyrical abstraction. I invite the world's great thinkers to reflect on this question, which should come into its own with the eradication of diseases and the democratisation of longevity. For the engineers interested in working on the issue, I should point out that my brief is still in development. Because naturally, it would be out of the question to deprive ourselves of all the various celebrations linked to different dates that we've become accustomed to. Our opportunities to get together and get outrageously, happily sloshed at the drop of a hat.

Age differences

O genie of the lamp, let the man of my life be the same age as me. Or if not, then younger.

I have the feeling that the issue of age difference has never loomed as large as it does in our fifties. When we learn that one of our male friends has 'met someone', the question that automatically follows is: 'How old is she?' Of course, we know the answer threatens to crucify the woman who asks, even though the unspoken hope is that it will be: 'They're the same age.'

Or the height of ecstasy: 'I think he's younger than her.'

Do men in their fifties prefer young women?

Men in their fifties want love and peace, or rather peace and love. They've been through war or boredom and are more interested in calm and compatibility. Most of them have hung up their vanity, and even though they don't all want the same thing, they're crystal clear about the points where they will no longer make concessions. Their divorces have given them new freedom and they won't make the same mistakes again.

Nevertheless, it's true that the young woman/older man configuration is more common, perhaps because men naturally succumb to a sort of primitive pride or reproductive instinct, who knows? With an older partner, a woman gains a particular power from her youth, almost a form of superiority, and sometimes commercial advantage. She doesn't experience worries over age, because she'll always be younger than him. On the other hand, she'll have to put on a brave face with her husband's doddery old friends, learn to die of boredom with a smile, and give up on things that she may regret later, when it's too late. Over time, everything she endures will loom larger and larger. Anyway, when you think about it, it's a funny thing to value a partner for her age, something we do nothing to deserve and can't control.

Physically, an age difference in excess of ten years seems to make the older of the two younger, but only at first – at the start of a relationship, when love has a direct and visible effect on your skin and your weight. Later, when passion goes into freefall and love's energy declines over the months and collapses over the years, things get worse. The grind of everyday life leads to sagging skin and the rictus of bitterness. He runs out of steam and refuses to show it. People will say he's 'well presented', like a crumpled figure in a starched suit. He may be on a slippery slope: first some tooth whitening or veneers, then a reduction of the goitre that his good friends will pretend not to have noticed, and finally a barrage of injections every six months that will make his face look like plastic.

These efforts to plug the leaks in a boat taking on water make a man or a woman determined to fight a losing battle against time look pathetic to other people. All these visible efforts will simply accentuate the age difference and make Mr Well-Presented look even older. But the thing people will notice most about him is his wife. Not her beauty though. They'll be looking out for the little signs of annoyance in her gestures or intonation, the unkind remarks and subtle reproaches, the things that she won't even try to hold back any more as the years go by. His trophy relationship was supposed to be a

34

source of pride for him, fulfilment for her, and envy for others; in the long run, all it will bring is disappointment for him, compassion from other people, and for her, at best a sort of fondness, at worst a self-serving attachment.

I admit to feeling a slightly shameful satisfaction at seeing an elderly gentleman dumped by his young girl-friend. 'Well done,' I always say to myself. And if the old man had previously left a wife in her fifties, it's all the sweeter.

Age differences the other way around

In contrast to the previous example, being with a younger man really is rejuvenating. The rhythm of life, the clothes, the way he talks, or doesn't, the way he laughs, and then in bed . . . the bedroom seals the deal. Impulsive sex, taut skin, alert muscles . . . And you get used to it, that's where things get complicated.

Socially, it's neither simple nor relaxed. Impulsive Sex will have friends his own age, with girlfriends who are perhaps even younger. Over time, it won't work out, and even less so with Junior's parents. Then it will depend on the family's influence and the friends' perceptions. Only a happy disposition coupled with a good dose of self-confidence will overcome this impression of living on borrowed time. And we shouldn't underestimate how much it hurts to be left by the one we love, combined with the heartache of imagining it's because we're so old.

I detest the word 'cougar'. Like all French words ending in an 'ar' sound (*connard, salopard, crevard* . . .)*, the sound of it only brings associations of masculine insults. This sexist term is extremely unfair: a cougar is a brave heroine who takes risks and responsibility for them. Since the last presidential election in France, the word has strangely fallen out of circulation, relegated to the realm of the politically incorrect, like any other judgement of a person based on their preferences. Our First Lady has certainly helped dispel the taboo surrounding this type of relationship, adding support to the idea that when it comes to desire, relationships and love, there is no such thing as normality. Women are much more relaxed about their age than before and now have the ultimate threat at their disposal: 'If you make me unhappy, I'll leave you for a French president twenty-four years my junior'.

Clearly, the ideal formula for staying afloat, besides love and understanding, is to share your life with a partner of the same generation, so that neither of you is the other's accessory, but instead their principality.

---

* Jerk, bastard, skinflint.

Unfortunately, available men of our age aren't running round the streets with a sign strapped to their stomachs, they're more likely well hidden under a rock. The problem for single women in their fifties is that it's easier to fish from the volcanic pool of younger men, or the less hot-blooded selection of older men. Those of the same age are already taken or not worth having.

I don't want to come over difficult, but I find most of the men my age a tiny bit too middle-aged for my taste. And then if they drink or work too much, and forget to take care of themselves, all of a sudden, they're in the category marked 'over the hill'. Not to forget the twin threats of baldness and belly fat. I won't dwell on the final, less visible problem, which has to be the one that worries us the most.

In contrast, I have the impression that fifty-something women are generally better preserved than their male counterparts. They can skilfully deal with the signs of age with methods that men are afraid of using without overshadowing their virility.

If a fifty-something is lucky enough to come across the rare treasure that is an unattached man of the same age, that's fantastic! In the best case, he'll be like her, intact and in a good state of repair. At worst, she'll start steaming his food and buy a comb (implying that she hadn't noticed). All with the proviso that he's not a layabout, that he can stand up straight and his professional life has left him comfortable and with high standards. Of course, he might give into the temptation of putting a pretty young doll on his arm. Perhaps he will.

Patience. He'll get over it. He'll come back.

One windy day, he'll be back on the market, stronger for the experience, cooled off by its consequences, ready to experience something different and finally mature enough for a relationship with no ulterior motives, sweet-natured and far removed from urban conceits – and another woman will snap him up.

Age overcome, age dealt with, age ignored, age eradicated!

Now that we're agreed that age is a detail of history, all we have to do is convince other people. And ultimately, convincing just one person would be enough.

In the meantime, the fledgling young fifty-something will have to face up to major upheavals and give her working surface a good wash down, leaving her serene at the prospect of a new equilibrium and, why not, the possibility of a man in her life.

Fifty and Single Again

Your major life choices have long since been made. You've had children or not, you're still in a relationship or not. At fifty, whatever you've done with your life, the cards have been shuffled. Of course, if you had a good run in Season 1, so much the better. But don't forget that Season 2 is even more promising. Between the two is a crucial decompression chamber. What this entails is up to you: time, freedom, light-heartedness, a few hook-ups for the experience that you'll pretend to regret but will actually do you good and send you on your way.

Being a single woman and being in your fifties are minor things individually but together weigh heavily at a time when psychological balance is difficult to achieve and easy to lose. Being on your own at fifty is much more of a delicate issue than at any other time of your life. Being newly single is distressing because it requires a change of habits, and changing things that have been engrained for years is always going to hurt. Our habits have laid down a soft bed of sediment and we need to force ourselves to see things in a new way on neutral ground without regretting what we once had.

Change is something you embrace at thirty. Change at fifty is something you're forced to get used to. It's OK to change for the 'better': a bigger apartment, a more comfortable bed or a better paid job. But change that brings unwelcome solitude, having breakfast on your own, falling asleep without a shoulder to snuggle up to and parting company with your ex's friends is truly awful. Nevertheless, if you take the trouble to look up at the horizon, you'll already be able to see the freedom and serenity that await. At this point, of course, you'll refuse to see it – or to believe your good friends who swear it's true. And yet . . .

Heartaches

Not only have you been dumped, but your former partner's family has also made it clear your presence is not welcome, even though you were a frequent guest until recently. The new government is planning a clear-out. For those who still have teenage children, the cruelty of the situation will mean they prefer to holiday at the ex's big family home, with the cousins, dogs, cats and grandparents. Leaving you alone and depressed.

For those who've been on their own for some time, being single isn't so complicated. These women's love lives have taken them through one door, then another, until they find themselves having to take a position: dynamic or safe, as the advisor at your bank might say when presenting his portfolio of financial products. As they've always done, these fifty-somethings will keep swimming in the deep end, finding love 'by surprise, on the move', and from time to time going back to the same old lovers, the ones who don't count, whom you never talk about, but who are there, and come when you whistle.

But of course, that's for the most optimistic, the most carefree, the boldest, the toughest. Those who have been through torrid relationships that are well and truly over won't really be interested in going there again.

Never again

The end of a relationship very often leaves you worn out, bitter and vulnerable, and some of us, having only just recovered from our break-ups, have told ourselves we will never fall for anything or anyone again. That we will keep love and its butterflies in the stomach at arm's length. That no one will be planting any flags anywhere after a battle of emotions. That going back anytime soon is out of the question.

Our faltering fifties are the time of life when we can coldly decide to cut out our capacity to love. By eradicating the idea of Love, couldn't we keep heartache at bay? Never being in love again should make life simpler. So it's out with Love. Get thee behind me, Love. Goodbye Love. In future, we will keep this emotional energy for the only person who deserves it: ourself.

And to avoid finding ourselves in the firing line of a distracted Cupid, we can always turn this decision into a work of art. One of my ideas for a performance piece (as yet untested) would be to hold a ceremony, place Love in a cloth, tie it up, dig a hole in the garden, bury the knotted cloth, plant a tree on top, scatter a few stones and maybe even put up a cross: 'Here lies Love'. Once Love has been shut away, we will finally be able to move on (we think). Work on our personal or professional plans, take a course in something or other, write a novel, learn book-binding, start a blog, read (or reread) the classics, take up Latin again, sign up for DIY workshops, jump off a bridge with one foot tied to an elastic band . . .

To live!

More than ever, at fifty, you only live once.

To live unencumbered, without waiting, without hoping . . .

Or that's what you'd like to believe at that moment.

Adopting a cat

O genie of the lamp, may I never feel the need to have a cat.

Cats are good companions, particularly for women. But after a certain age, and depending on circumstances, they can be much more than that: an allied presence, a fresh perspective, a source of easy-going relativism, a day-to-day partner and a kindly ear.

The life expectancy of my relationship with my cat has often been longer than with my husbands and lovers.

Perhaps because he never asks for anything and seems to be satisfied with everything. He unstintingly provides balance and affection, in the same way as plants bring peace and contemplation.

Cats demand not just attention but love. And we have such a great need to distribute love, particularly when our homes are emptying out. So with no one else in the frame, the cat becomes a transitional object, picking up the crumbs of your love and filling the empty space in your life, your living room and your heart.

This is how, on the threshold of my fifties and at the end of a love story, I found myself welcoming in the adorable little ball of fur that my daughter had decided to give me without asking. She herself was struggling with adolescence, which had come far too soon for my taste, and was taking too much advantage of an unbridled freedom, with a suspected side order of illicit substances. At what point did she think to herself that the presence of a cat would distract me from her own transgressions? Suffice it to say that if she'd asked me if I wanted a cat I would have screamed 'Out of the question!', but when she turned up carrying a three-week-old kitten with a red ribbon round his neck, I immediately turned into marshmallow.

As soon as Pouppy came into my life, I felt good (well, better, let's not exaggerate). Wherever I went in the apartment, he followed me, sitting down next to me, becoming part of the décor and content with simply being there. I was enchanted when he snuggled up to me and I felt his raspy tongue on my neck, all for the price of some cat food and a clean litter tray. Sometimes, his effusiveness was too much – one-sided love can be a real burden! So I would send him away more or less gently according to my mood at the time, but he never held it against me, and seemed to forget the incident a second afterwards. Later, with his typically feline quiet calm, he would come back as if nothing had happened (every woman's dream).

I quickly realised, however, that his slightest defect was his gender, and he lost no time in making himself at home with my designer furniture, which has the claw marks to prove it. He also regularly succumbed to lapses of control on the velvet of my sofa, before smiling up at me, or at least that's what I thought I could read in his expression. What was the answer? In New York, they would have recommended a pet therapist. But I live in Paris. So whilst I found the idea of robbing him of his virility distressing, with these events repeating on an almost daily basis, castration appeared to be the inevitable solution. Afterwards, his arrogance disappeared, and I began to grow much fonder of the calmer cat he'd become. His incredible change was more compatible with my Dyptique candles and the preservation of my personal environment.

Break-ups

Everyone complains of the burden that fate has imposed on them. But not in the same way. Some shed their burden after a short and discreet waiting period, happy to have short memories. Others bear the weight of their suffering to the end of their lives and constantly return to it in conversation. Obsessions set up camp in their brains like an incurable virus.

How to advise a friend after a break-up

Is a break-up always the end of the world? Let's explore the positive sides. He's gone, true, but he hasn't left you; he's set you free.

Remember your friend's infinite patience when you were in a mess, and the way you wanted to slap her when she quite rightly told you: 'Look at the positives, you're free now'?

Well, now it's your turn, because your dear friend has come to you to give you the full rundown of her marital misadventures. With her head almost underwater, she's trying to heave herself clumsily over the side of the boat even though that bastard has pulled up the ladder and set sail. For some time, her husband had been screwing around – we all knew it, even her, despite her denial. He hesitated, but now he's gone. So how can you respond, what can you say, what can you do?

Start off with an indignant '*No!* Not him, I don't believe it', even if you're only half surprised by the news. The delayed mirror effect makes you realise how much you must have bent her ear back then about the idiot whose name you've thankfully now forgotten. You should remind her about the time she devoted to you, say thank you and apologise. But whilst playing this virtual joker, you must return the favour and listen attentively for as long as she wants, with the same pseudo-empathy she once showed you.

As you think of potential distractions from her woes, start by trying to comfort her with a whole barrage of enlightened advice. Safe in the knowledge it's all pointless because the wall in front of you is impenetrable. Warnings and analysis are useless because she won't hear anything, especially anything that might go against what she's telling you. So you just listen, feigning positivity with suggestions that she moves forward, sees people, gets some exercise, has a massage, signs up to a dating site, breathes, meditates . . . and perhaps even goes to bed with one of those anonymous peacock-like lotharios who are always hanging around when you go out in town. Although this last suggestion would be very effective and uplifting, she'll reply (as you knew she would) that she just couldn't.

You'll put a lot of effort into trying to find what you think are the right words. But don't take too much trouble, as it will all go unnoticed or fall flat. So stick to the facts, don't judge, stir things up, imagine, extrapolate, over-interpret or get carried away. Rein in your emotions, try to soothe hers and above all, don't indulge in any criticism, because naturally, before they permanently go their separate ways, they'll sleep together a few more times.

Your good friend won't tell you she's seeing him again, and like a good friend, you'll hide your suspicions. She won't follow any of your strategic advice and she'll do just what she wants. But why, I hear you ask? So did you listen to her advice then? My advice is never to get mixed up in other people's relationships: emotional or sexual impulses will always trump your good intentions.

And the end result will still be the same: one more single woman in an already crowded marketplace.

Don't complain

The whole bed to yourself, oil in your hair at night, moisturiser in your socks, one weekend in two with no kids, all those kilos that no diet would ever have shifted, nights out on the spur of the moment and a field of possibilities opening up to you after long years of married life!

So go on, cut short your mourning, empty the basket, look at the advantages of this new existence, change channel and say thank you to life. Governments may change, but we will always be there, the good friends with the words and ideas to transform powerlessness through our goodwill.

Did you know that there are natural antidotes to sadness just as there are natural enemies of bad cholesterol (pineapple, for example)? Over a good bottle of Saint-Julien, we'll tell you about them. And also you should read, as reading really is a palliative for heartache.

There are two possible options.

The first is to read about terrible things that make you think: 'There are people a lot worse off than me, so I shouldn't complain'. A humiliating break-up, losing a job, losing a loved one, a heart transplant, cancer, basically heart-rending real-life experiences that leave you telling yourself you're lucky to be alive.

The other strategy is to read positive, joyful things. But also to watch comedies and harness the power of laughter to spread optimism.

It's your choice, but I recommend the second option.

Keep your dignity!

The end of a relationship should be discreet. I'm always fascinated by women who fight to the point of indignity to keep their man (and their status). Their belligerence is sometimes rewarded, but at what price? What doesn't kill love never makes it stronger, just more precarious. You feel like telling them to let go, to end things elegantly, to unlock their jaws and not to spit venom, even though it's hard to lose your place so quickly, with no warning or golden parachute. Except it's the only outcome. So tip-toe away, my dear, look elsewhere, to your future, the one you'll invent for yourself. Take control, don't endure. Even try smiling. No, not that terrifying forced smile with all the teeth, the other, detached smile. Wish him the best. Be classy! Of course, you'll have to deal with your heartache, that's the way it is! But don't rant about your rival's faults, her crooked teeth, her squint, her stupidity and her lurid past. It's useless. Bringing her down won't raise you up. Even so, there will be things to say about her, as he'll discover pretty soon. So swallow your barbs and disappear, head held high. Take a trip to India and stop off for an ayurvedic retreat in Kerala. You'll see, you'll come back (or not) transformed, with your chakras open.

And then one day.

You'll have her in your sights.

Your finger on the trigger.

You won't waver.

Fifty-somethings in single mode

We have no other option than to make the best of this new solitude. Women who become single without planning to discover the drawbacks at a late stage. You only realise the benefits long after that.

At first, you'll make it clear to whoever will listen that you're absolutely fine with it, enjoying your freedom, and wouldn't want to share your bed or your life with a full-timer for anything.

'Hell, no!' you say, generally adding, 'I've suffered enough.'

For most of you, this may well not be true. Why? Because your cherished freedom conceals a secret aspiration for everything you claim to dismiss: living together, a joint lease on an apartment, sharing the laundry basket and receiving invitations written in the plural. You say you're done with all that? Perhaps it's just a posture.

Because if one day you meet someone you like, why not share a plate of pasta and a glass of Chardonnay with him on one of those slightly damp, depressing Sunday evenings?

After all the battering our hearts have taken, when we'd wrapped them in cloth and buried them in the garden, what if we went and dug them up?

We're talking about Love!

Because everyone, or everyone who hasn't found it already, is looking for Love. Love is the most important thing, so come on, let's give it a capital letter. OK, so someone will always say 'first health, then love' when the subject comes up. Well, no, health doesn't get a capital letter. And outside of marginal cultural phenomena like TV series with a medical theme or bestsellers focusing on organs with little poetic potential, literature and cinema have a lot more to say about Love than health. Most of the time, Love and nothing else is what makes you a little bit beautiful, a little bit strong or a little bit dead. Love is the cause; good or bad health is the consequence. So what colour of Love will it be?

Looking for love, or the season of rejection

The many colours of love

Every love 'match' is unique, it imprints its own colour, and our little hearts deal with this diversity as best they can, despite the experiences and useless scars that ultimately don't teach us a great deal. There are many colours of Love, and each age has its own trend. At fifty, after living through grey skies and rainbows, we can hold up a wet finger and very quickly tell if the temperature is right, if the winds are against us or turning, and if our heart's little paintbrush will be dipped into the bright colours of passion or the darkness of the long tunnel that comes from going down the wrong track.

Were we able to deal with things when they happened? Will we be able to see more clearly now that we know the rules? How do we deal with the pitfalls? Monotony, betrayal, itchy feet?

The solution is to find the right one.

Or to have found the right ones.

At the right time.

There's a broad palette of different kinds of love. Mellow Love that patches you up or stays with you for the long haul; co-dependent Love that engulfs and leaves you weary; platonic Love that doesn't engulf you enough and also leaves you weary, belligerent; compulsive Love based only on neurosis; indifferent Love that flatters the pride; toxic Love that wreaks havoc on those who keep coming back; passionate Love that helps you lose weight; self-interested Love that helps you accumulate pension contributions; destructive Love that avenges childhood suffering; nostalgic Love that reminds us of our past mistakes; hormone-induced sexual Love for recreation or paid for by the hour; Love by correspondence, in which each party wields a pen and keeps desire at arm's length; sad Love; mad Love; gay Love; casual Love, which isn't so common after a certain age; 'for ever' Love, reserved for those we've lost; awakening Love, which makes you look and feel better; dying Love, which leaves you bitter and makes you feel worse; Love near and far; wild Love; gentle Love. In short, not one but many.

So where do you find the right one? Who has that in stock?

In my most pessimistic moments, I do the following calculation: if you remove married men from the pool of possibilities, as well as those who have remade their lives with young women, those who prefer men, those who've been permanently put off by their divorces, those who've been hooked in by religion, those who will only ever love their mothers, those who've become impotent and would rather no one found out, those who turn out to be transgender or genetically modified, how many are left for a nice young single fifty-something? And given this shortage, should we steal a man from someone else? Hope other people's relationships break down? Learn shamanism or, better still, the art of solitude?

New Year's Eve

31 December is an occasion that reawakens the trauma of unwelcome single status. You've agreed to go to a party where you don't know anyone. It gets off to a bad start when you bump into a bombshell with 120-centimetre legs in the lift. She's stunning, and after exchanging a few words, you discover that the game pâté in her bag is home-made, from game she hunted herself, at her own château. If there's a half-decent single man around, she'll be the winner. And if she follows the Champions League, you really are in trouble.

But for the real killer blow, you have to wait for the countdown to midnight. That's when you realise you're alone, and not just metaphysically.

5, 4, 3, 2, 1.

Happy New Year.

The couples kiss and wish one another health and happiness. These few minutes are the worst. There you are, sitting on your hands, filled with a desire to disappear deep into the floor and not come back out. It's a bad start to the year, and you watch the bombshell with the château dancing uninhibitedly, squeezed into the wide belt she's wearing as a skirt. She seems happy, aware of her beauty, and the men are watching her. There's no chance they'll notice you, on the other hand, down there in the floor.

So for a long time, I resigned myself to spending the night of the 31st in bed, to spare myself the five minutes before and after midnight. It's an evening that inspires dejection more than the joy of sharing. Why am I alone amongst these other couples?

It's in your head! What if the bombshell had more reasons than you to be desperate?

If you can't control what you feel, you can always do something about your image, your clothes and your smile. The levers we can control all provide positive solutions to help us maintain a good self-image, which is something at least. The rest usually follows. So we should be sure to stabilise our weight, to be well dressed, well styled and well descaled, to smile, accept all kinds of invitations, invent some lovers, and actually have some.

On this last point, I've noticed that certain single women

in their fifties, mainly those with a healthy ego, are happy to boast about their numerous conquests. I find it funny because these are the same women who, at thirty, tried every trick in the book to conceal their transgressions. Back then, there was a lot of action and no talk, now I wonder if there's as much action as they make out. But that's beside the point. After all, what counts is looking like a seductress. It's about showing willing.

Don't rush in

Your search engine is in place, and everyone can see you flashing your headlights (male and female, rest assured), but as your criteria have grown stricter over the years, this has considerably cut down the field of possibilities. So where are you going to give ground? Sure, you'll agree to make a few concessions, but how far will you go? Average looks? A gaggle of children? Cash flow issues? Dubious manners? A low coefficient of penile expansion? Deviant techniques?

It will be easy to indulge his little obsessions or insignificant defects, but when your love for him comes up against the limits of what you will accept, you might legitimately say to yourself: a man, yes, but not just any man, and not at any price.

So set yourself up with a retinal scanner and examine everything that walks by your windows. Leave the radar permanently on, and take your time, without preconceptions or judgement. And above all, in spite of your red lines, try to be indulgent.

I'm handing out advice here like I know what I'm talking about, but just as psychiatrists are notoriously unstable and teachers' kids do badly at school, there I was turning over dark thoughts in my mind, stuck in a bed I shared with a poor cat. Hello, positive thinking.

At that point I had a wake-up call and decided to change gears and go into conquest mode. I would put on my battle gear and set myself up to meet someone. In any case, I promised myself I wouldn't be spending another New Year's Eve alone with a cat.

'NEVER AGAIN!' I said to the cat, plunging my head into a box of tissues.

The time for discouragement was over, but the season of rejection was just beginning.

'See you at home!'

I remember one man I met in a restaurant. He was handsome (beauty is important), and was eating alone at the bar. I was next to him, with a girlfriend. The perfect set-up for a nice little conversation. First, we swapped smiles, then phone numbers. Later, I found out he wasn't free, but as soon as he was, two months later, he called me. It was a classic start: exhibition, dinner, bed. We woke up and were in second gear, and the day after, I had the impression that we'd slipped straight into third. Anyway, a bit too quickly for my taste, something told me we were heading full speed into a full-blown relationship. I like things to go slowly, especially when I'm not in the driving seat. But how do you stop a racing machine without the risk of breaking the spell with this prince charming you've spent so long trying to meet?

It was a few words that lit the fuse that sent me running. As my handsome friend was living in an attic room with a shared bathroom in the dodgy bit of the 17th arrondissement, we hadn't considered anywhere but my place for our frolics. On the third day of our idyllic relationship, he called me at around six-thirty. 'Darling, I've bought some bread,' he said with great affection, 'will I see you at home?'

First of all, he'd called me 'darling' (which I'd never taken to despite years of marriage), and then, prince charming was inviting himself over, apparently for dinner. The implication of bringing the bread was that it would have been a nice gesture for me to make a little starter and after that, why not the main course, then for dessert, who knows?

Finally, that 'see you at home' left me wondering.

'At home? But whose home?'

'You know, at home . . . at home, your place!'

Silence. Awkwardness. What was he thinking? What was I doing with him?

Which species were living in the backwater of available men? How many alligators was I going to meet before I found someone who would start out at the right tempo? Who would leave time for an approach, for seduction, for reflection, and for distance as well. In short, the time it takes to learn a little bit about the other person. The time we allow for desire to gently build.

This is the problem with independent women: the men who fall into their beds are too easy. If you find yourself going through a difficult time with no psychological support besides a daily dose of Effexor and a cat, there's a high risk of succumbing to a man in a tight spot who offers you love in exchange for pooling your possessions and finances. And before you know it, you'll find yourself pushing an Ikea trolley with him. The stuff of nightmares.

While taking a similar tranquiliser, a talented male friend of mine, who's rich and handsome to boot, got married very quickly to a gold-digger, who was identified as such by all his male friends (who were horrified), by his female friends (who were distraught) and even by the gold-digger herself (who was over the moon). The day he stopped his medication, he discovered a difficult woman, who had little in common with him culturally, who'd moved her two young children into his apartment along with her furniture, and had a third on the way. In circumstances like those, it's very difficult to back-pedal, and I can't help thinking he ought to have sued the company that makes the antidepressant.

So don't worry, repeating your mistakes is entirely normal. Everyone does it, I can assure you. Each failure increases your suspicion and distrust, but never give up. You'll develop a certain frivolity, out of necessity rather than choice, with the sad realisation that the available men still on the market don't match up to the men in your dreams.

You'll ultimately be forced to conclude that the 'best' men have already been spoken for, for some time. You'll grind your teeth at the sight of certain wives who are unappreciative on every level, and permit themselves to mistreat the kind and charming husbands by their sides, if possible in front of witnesses. Why are the most thoughtful men often in relationships with harridans who bully them as soon as they get the opportunity? Perhaps simply because these women picked them out, helped themselves first and spotted the neurosis that would intertwine with their own. You know the ones, the type that takes up all the room in a photo. That's her! Brazen, used to attention, sure of herself and unaware of the mismatch.

With a bit of the bar-room psychology we like to indulge in, we could look to the father in her case.

In his case, the mother.

Should you revise your criteria downwards? Your minimum standards might start to erode as you come to terms with the scarcity of the product on the crisis-hit market. My advice: set the bar high, but cast a wide net.

A disastrous man. Season 1

My default type is a paunchy Mediterranean with lots of dark hair. I like cuddly, shaggy teddy bears with a bit of meat on them. Don't ask me why, that's just how it is. I have no explanation for this preference, which is in no way oedipal because neither my father nor my mother look like that. So when a bald guy over six feet tall offered to take me to the theatre, the reason I said yes was because he'd written the play.

That first evening, my lofty playwright watched me laughing out of the corner of his eye, before taking me to dinner, during which we revealed only what seduction, mystery and propriety allowed on a first date. The smiles were genuine, the conversation flowed, and everything went well enough for us to make a second date there and then, followed by a third. I liked him.

He revealed some excellent qualities – humour, kindness, modesty – things in short supply when you live in Paris, and behind his triangular grey eyes and soft voice was the sophisticated tortuousness of a brilliant mind. But what seduced me above all was his gentle nature.

At this stage and at our age, if two people like each other, they go for it. There's an academic and social process that follows a timescale ranging from one day (or one night) to six months or more (depending on their boldness and affinity), during which they see each other, talk and go out, all whilst waiting for the crucial moment that will reveal the existence or absence of sexual compatibility.

But things dragged on, and each time we performed our cultural or gastronomic rituals, I found myself coordinating my underwear, telling myself that perhaps, that night, who knows . . .

But no, nothing happened.

Each time we met, I was plunged further and further into a state of nervousness, as feelings of confusion set in. In spite of myself, I clumsily developed a counterproductive strategy of unjustified silences. Quite presumptuously, I waited for my beau to go down on one knee with a rose in his hand. Nothing of the sort happened. He didn't reveal himself by word or deed, only by omission. I felt he was completely blocked, and wondered if he'd been devastated by his recent separation. In complete disarray, I spoke to my friend Nicolas, who knows a thing about complex relationships. He agreed to act as my coach.

'He's a broken man, barely still on his feet.'

The explanation suited me, since every woman looking for love has a nurse lying dormant in her heart.

So Nicolas and I analysed his texts and emails and thought about the phrasing to use in replies with just one aim in mind: to close the (bloody) deal. All our efforts were in vain.

It had been three months since our first meeting and nothing had happened. My coach had had enough.

The man was slow.

Or not interested.

Not interested, said the coach, forget it.

But one day, when I was saying goodbye, I went up on tip-toes to kiss him on the cheek, forgetting to completely turn my head, and I felt that this was the moment, something was going to happen.

So he took the plunge and, finally, kissed me! But no tongue and hands behind his back, which is neither relaxing nor inspiring. Such clumsiness left me paralysed. I sensed he was shut off, unavailable.

So to restore my self-confidence, I distracted myself a little, just enough to carry on seeing him with a smile on my face.

He doesn't want me, but never mind.

He doesn't know what he's missing.

I love being single, I'm free, I have my life in front of me.

At least that's what I told myself, with tears in my eyes and my nose in a tissue.

With the girls

In this period of single existence, when the excess of freedom is both anxiety-forming and all-pervading, your friends are mainly girlfriends. We meet up with the girls to share moans, alcohol and stories. What difference is there between our preoccupations and those of a bunch of thirty-somethings? Almost none.

'Masculine and feminine are growing further apart, and before long, we'll have a war between men and women.' This from Virginie, fifty-four, two kids, man trouble for the past five years.

'War?'

'That's right, men are our enemies. Either we fight, or they go.'

'Can someone explain this? Come on girls, Virginie's having a breakdown!'

'Look around you, where are the men? There aren't any,' she replied.

But fear not, Virginie immediately abandoned the idea of a war (along with her friends) when she found what she was looking for. One day, pfft, she disappeared. I don't know if she won the war, but she found peace . . . and a man.

A disastrous man, Season 2

I'd been single for too long. Not unhappy, but single. I told myself that to find a man, I had to go out to parties and dinners and keep my eyes wide open. And the best way to pick up some invitations, is to throw your own party. So the invitations were sent out: save the date messages to my whole address book. Everyone would bring along a bottle and whoever they wanted. I added a smiley, and off they went.

Naturally, my guest list included that beanpole of a man whom I had such as soft spot for despite his baldness and his fumbling lips. He asked me if he could come with his friend Dominique, who was visiting Paris from the south of France.

'No problem,' I said, 'bring who you like. I'm making tarts.'

'Tarts?' he said.

'Yes, I make tarts to die for,' I replied proudly.

I didn't know at this point that I'd be the one wanting to die by the end of the evening.

I invited about twenty people. Everything was ready, and the entry phone rang. It was him. He was the first guest. They were the first. I opened the door. For two seconds, I imagined he'd run into the pretty woman beside him in the lift and she'd got the wrong floor. And then they both smiled at me. He handed me a bottle. She held out her hand.

Dominique turned out to be a stunning brunette who must have been born around the year I turned fifteen. She lived in Nice, where she worked as an anaesthetist. In three minutes and a few sentences, I was devastated. If she'd been beautiful but dim, with a tiny physical defect, it would have been less painful, or if she'd at least had an embarrassing accent . . . but not even that!

I screwed a smile to my (anaesthetised) face and ran to fill my glass. He has the right to prefer a younger woman, I told myself. After all, he's not the first, nor the only one. But that evening, watching the two of them dance, it was also my right to conclude, with a half-smile, that they weren't right together. He was making too much effort to be thoughtful, she wasn't doing enough to tone herself down. And she left a whiff of 'too much' in her wake: too much perfume, too tanned, too many cigarettes . . .

But perhaps I was simply a bit too jealous?

My coach came over and, always ready with a smart remark, whispered to me: 'Well, his anaesthetist has certainly put him under!'

I picked myself up and sharpened my claws.

'But what's she got that I haven't?'

'Oh, nothing. She's just fifteen years younger.'

I was devastated, but at least the situation was clear. And I had more proof that things happen quickly or not at all.

After the party, someone handed me a joint the size of a chocolate éclair. I hadn't touched my tarts and I'd drunk everything in sight. The grass finished me off. My vomit hit the living room wall in a horizontal trajectory, splattering over a final guest who was even drunker than I was.

I took three days to recover from that evening, lying immobile in my bed, eyes glued to the screen of my phone, with its string of thank-yous tinged with compassion. How had this happened to me, former queen of the night and breaker of hearts?

He called me.

I didn't answer.

I wasn't in the mood to hear his excuses.

Finally, I resolved to listen to his message. He'd phoned to tell me what a lovely evening it had been.

With no certificate of youth, I decided to focus on three things: imagination (wit, frivolity, joy, self-deprecation . . .), elegance (outfits, look, poise . . .) and hoping my opponent would mess up, because even though I was throwing in the towel . . . who knew if Miss Côte d'Azur might put the odd foot wrong. First and foremost, did she have enough of a sense of humour? He wasn't going to make any concessions there. Every man has his criteria, which he weights according to his preferences. For this gentle soul, with his finely honed wisecracks and almost permanent air of semi-depression, humour was a necessity, almost a way of life, helping him to deal with an intrinsic, structural seriousness. Nothing I would object to, but in the meantime, I was struggling to deal with the rejection.

I've always noticed that the younger and prettier a woman is, the more she permits herself to show defects that would be unacceptable in your fifties. Affectations and whims, for example, sit better with freshness of youth and its accompanying smile. Similarly, men can forgive the young and beautiful for a lack of culture, the absence of kindness, a sense of humour bypass, non-existent generosity, an empty CV and an empty bank account. Thanks to the principle of compensation.

At the same time, due to the urgent need for a rapid restoration of my battered ego, I signed up for some sessions with a local therapist. She advised me to put my flashers on, in other words besides going out and inviting people round for tarts, I should be more direct, and make my interest clearer to the men around me. Which I did.

Ghosting

The first to spot my flashing lights was Édouard. He was young and handsome, with the sort of piercing wit I appreciate and the kind of dangerous intelligence I worry about. I met him at a dinner, at the end of which I started dancing exuberantly, almost wildly. I imagine this was my idea of flashing lights: smiling and dancing. In any case, the method worked. Two days later, despite not having asked for my number, he called me, revealing a funny, generous side.

He was determined to take me to a dream destination for a weekend away. We talked about the most romantic Italian cities but couldn't decide. One day, we were discussing the choice with one of his friends who'd lived in Italy, and I almost bashfully suggested Lake Como, which is my idea of an ultimate romantic bolthole, like any lake for that matter. The friend's response to my suggestion was that it was an extremely boring place, so you'd have to be very much in love. To which Édouard came straight back with: 'Well, we'd best be quick then.'

Do I appreciate these witty remarks as much when they're at my expense? A little less, I think. The good sport in me clashed with the armour of my ego. In any event, my loveable bastard didn't know how right he was.

Of course, I should have got up and left. But just after saying something humiliating (this wasn't the only example!), he knew how to make himself adorable. A hot/cold technique that could drive you crazy. After three months of this on and off behaviour, and just before the famous romantic weekend was due to go ahead, Édouard suddenly vanished. Radio silence.

This behaviour linked to new technology is known as ghosting. One day, someone disappears from your radar screens. You can no longer reach them, and they never call. You're amazed at their silence and send a question mark, but with no reply forthcoming, you realise it's actually a full stop. It's a cowardly approach, but effective, annoying or even traumatising for the person on the receiving end. No embarrassing sobs, no tearful last meal, no 'you're a really wonderful person, you know', just before the plate of *spaghetti alle vongole* ends up down someone's front, no 'you deserve better', which goes hand in hand with 'our relationship couldn't tolerate mediocrity'. No clumsy explanations – 'I don't love you enough' – or complicated ones – 'I just don't feel right'. No.

Just a smartphone function: 'block sender'.

A long time later, I received a text from Édouard: 'How are you?' In classic text speak, that means: 'I'm not doing so well. Got some stuff to tell you.' But coming from an ex, it's more like, 'When are we going to get it on again?' Perhaps in a period of famine and oppressive solitude, I would have replied: 'Good, and you?' and we would have re-embarked on an occasional, precarious, soul-destroying relationship. Did I have the defences to be messed around like that again? To avoid having to ask the question, I immediately deleted his text/sext and emptied the trash.

Time to hold our heads high!

The advantages of being/dating a young fifty-something

In terms of the purely intuitive statistics drawn from my personal contacts, I have the impression that we young single women of the female persuasion on the cusp of our fifties and beyond come equipped with certain advantages and are finally reaping the benefits. To give myself a boost after everything I'd been through, I set about writing the fairly generic list below, which can be personalised according to your individual profile.

Children

By now, you've had your children. With a bit of luck, they've already grown up and, with even more luck, left home. And for the cherry on the cake, they're already standing on their own two feet.

The assurance that their existence is not too much of a drain on our income brings with it peace of mind, alongside the certainty of knowing they're in good health. And to remove any remaining guilt, psychoanalysis has taught us that their personal fulfilment was dependent on cutting ties with their parents, and that even disagreements and arguments were entirely desirable for their mental development. The fact that the file is closed in no way dilutes the pleasure of seeing them when we invite them over for Sunday lunch.

This only applies if the children were conceived around the generally accepted legal age, in other words somewhere in the region of thirty. Things are changing now, given the trend amongst forty-somethings to want to (and be able to) have children later in life. Which will considerably alter the agenda for young fifty-somethings fifteen years down the line. In New York, young single women of thirty-five and over with at least 20,000 dollars to spare are having their eggs frozen, so as to be less stressed about their biological clocks and give them time to find 'the one'. An ethically dubious procedure that could well reach our own shores before long. I can imagine a sixty-year-old with her box of eggs in the freezer suggesting to her partner that they combine their gametes to have a baby. After all, who knows if sixty might become the new thirty? But I'm launching a solemn appeal to medical researchers: please put an expiry date on the box, because I sense that some women might lose the plot:

'Hello, what's your name? And who's this little boy? Is he your brother?'

'No, that's granny's son!'

Work

In career terms, the die has generally been cast. We are no longer competing against anyone and our weapons have been laid at the feet of our most single-minded colleagues. Having reached the high point of our careers, we've been able to leave behind the concentrated stress that got us there. No need to be hustlers when we've already made it. Our egos retracted very slightly when we learnt that the thirty-year-old in the office next door had been taken on at the same salary because she 'had more experience on the digital side'. Which has the disadvantage of being unfair, irritating and logical.

Perhaps you came up against the glass ceiling and stagnated in the backwaters of an uneventful job, which paid an uneventful salary and led to an uneventful social life? Or maybe you're one of those who burst through that glass ceiling? Brandishing your taser, you dare them to try to block the path of a big game hunter like you, or encourage you to retire. Bring it on!

Money

The financial advantage of fifty-somethings, somewhere between a roof and a savings account, is the assurance that we've seemingly been able to match our needs to our assets, and so we shouldn't cost him too much – at any rate not as much as the previous regime, which left him rinsed, wrung out and in pieces.

Without wanting to belittle us, the 'maintenance' of a young fifty-something, as English speakers say about the upkeep of an apartment or a wife, should be less costly than for a budding thirty-something. Just a heads up to any skinflints, or those who have already had their fingers burnt.

Experience

We've acquired a full knowledge of the possible pitfalls in a relationship and have learnt some lessons as a result. Even though our neuroses are immune to the passing years, we can offer a suggestion of relative emotional security. Of course, there is no guarantee of results, nor after-sales service, especially as we have also acquired a number of habits unsuitable for sharing, but provided these are compatible with his, then bingo!

There is always a risk of failure, boredom or meeting someone else, and the dreadful possibility that you're on the receiving end. Being with someone you love means taking the risk of being left and getting hurt. But as we've been through it every which way, we're aware of this from the start.

In search of the perfect man

Now that we've reinflated our egos, let's try to protect ourselves from the collateral damage that romantic rejec-

tion can inflict on our moods, weight and skin. To avoid
wasting our increasingly precious time, it makes sense to
start by determining the profile of the perfect candidate
to spend our lives with – or at least a portion of our lives.

At sixteen, my perfect man had to be able to carve
through powder, and slalom on a water-ski. If he could
kick up a massive spray and knew the guitar chords
to Maxime Le Forestier's *San Francisco*, so much the
better. At twenty, I wanted a classical musician or a mav-
erick politician. At twenty-five, I would go for a classics
graduate from a top university or a professional golfer.
Someone to teach me things, give me books to read and
turn me into a sponge. At thirty, he had to have a clear
career plan, show fierce ambition in the most modest
way possible and agree without further comment when
I ranted about my father's attitude. At thirty-five, it was
preferable for him to be able to tell funny stories and
entertain the gallery. At forty, he had to be a virtuoso.
But in which field? Go on, have a guess!

No, not cooking.

No, not the slalom.

Think Serge Gainsbourg and Jane Birkin.

And at fifty, who do we dream of? Who is the perfect
man for a young fifty-something?

The perfect man is an ex

The relationship ended on a stupid pretext many years ago and your ex still remembers you when you were young and pert. You know each other, you knew each other, you liked each other, you know it works, the reasons it stopped working are no longer relevant, so why not? An ex saves time. Perhaps you could have lunch with him on a regular basis, so as to keep in contact, take the temperature, or simply to keep an eye on his current relationship. This contact will allow you to gauge an abstract possibility, something undefinable and reassuring, that you can file somewhere amongst the information in your mental 'cloud'. A sort of emotional fallout shelter. Your ex exists, hidden away somewhere, and that's good to know. After a certain age, starting up a new relationship isn't easy, but restarting an old one . . .

The perfect man is the same age as us

For preference, he should be someone from your own age bracket, which as we've seen, isn't always very easy to find when you're coming back to market quite late in the day. The advantage of belonging to the same generation is the sense of complicity, of being part of the same world, a shared emotional attachment to past events. It's being able to sing a song from *Atom Heart Mother* together. We know the old order, we've lived through the same revolutions. This shared understanding makes for some nice rallies. You can smash it into the corner, one bounce is all it takes, and the ball comes back.

In terms of health, a couple from the same generation share the same energy levels, similar periods of fatigue and down time, encroaching rheumatism, creaking joints, crumbling teeth, hearing loss, the discovery that whole sections of the masonry of our memory have collapsed . . . They are particularly sensitive to the other's needs and tolerant of the uncomfortable subjects we don't like to talk about – colonoscopy, hair loss, prostate, dental implants – which are outlawed in relationships with an age difference.

The perfect man is kind

Because kindness is fashionable and comes right at the top of the list of required qualities, the perfect man for a woman in her fifties is a nice guy. What we once took for weakness (they'll know who they are) has now acquired shades of absolute nobility. To be certain that your target possesses these qualities, you shouldn't hesitate to take a discreet look at his romantic biography. What state did he leave his exes in? First impressions can be supplemented by a few second opinions, but watch out for advisors and the light-fingered. If there's a perfect man knocking about, your rivals are bound to be prowling around him already, armed with a butterfly net.

The perfect man is seductive

He's not the most handsome, but you look at the perfect man and you like what you see. If he doesn't have all the aforementioned qualities, it's not too much of a problem. The fact that you fancy him alone cancels out certain qualities that you would never have imagined being able to overlook on an empty stomach. But even so, be sure to get your hands on the low-down of his services rendered. Seductiveness can be treacherous.

Sometimes, steering clear of a man who is too obviously appealing is a sensible course of action.

The perfect man is not on social media

He keeps his narcissism to himself. At worst, he's a passive user, at best, he's not on Facebook or Instagram and doesn't tweet either, because he's not involved in politics and doesn't have anything particular to sell. Nor is he on LinkedIn, because he's not looking for clients or for work. Firstly, he already has a job, and secondly, he knows very well that at his age (because he's the same age as you), that's not the way to go about finding one.

The perfect man has dealt with his problems

The perfect man is divorced. His past life is finished, digested and tidied away somewhere in the cellar. There's nothing worse than living to a schedule of delayed divorce-court rulings and maintenance payments still to be negotiated. For a long time, the perfect man went to bed early with the same woman. Perfection demands that she was the guilty party, who left him after time took its toll. Over the years, his wife became jaded, before running away overnight with a Togolese mechanic. Once the surprise had worn off, and the awareness that he too had been bored in their relationship had dawned, the perfect man was relieved. There's nothing worse than a marriage that loses its spark coupled with persistent bitterness. So he stayed good friends with his ex. The details of the divorce were settled over a good bottle in a local bistro with the division of assets scribbled down on the corner of the paper tablecloth, which they simply handed over to their shared lawyer. Nothing is more vulgar than endless war and complex calculations. The perfect man isn't at war with anyone, particularly his ex-wife. He hates conflict and pretends not to know how to count.

With the perfect man, the children come ready-made, better still already grown, and even better already out of the house. But if there are still any children nestling under his wings, what luck! Because just like the perfect man, his children are naturally kind, intelligent, charming, happy and independent, and also because walking around in the summer in denim shorts, with a straw hat, a bit of tinted cream on your nose, your perfect man on your arm and his young children following on behind, trailing the sweet misapprehension that they might be yours, is a young look, take my word for it.

The perfect man is a widower

On the face of it, I wouldn't have spontaneously come up with this target. We're cynical, yes, but like to keep things elegant. And yet a conversation with one of my friends got me thinking.

At fifty-five, Laurence had been single for three years. Her husband had upped and left after twenty-five years, the day after their last child got his degree results. Since then, he'd been writhing in the arms of a thirty-year-old Ukrainian. For her, it was as if he was dead, but even crueller. If he was dead, at least she'd have a pension, she told me half-seriously.

Shortly after, when it was her children's turn to leave, she told herself it was time to find a new companion. She went through the people she knew, in vain, and then spent a bit of time on a dating site. At first it was funny, then disappointing, and she ended up getting hurt several times. Between the eternal bachelors never ready to settle down, the men whose divorce will never be settled, and those who are still sleeping with their ex-wives, Laurence explained to me one evening that the market was paralysed, before triumphantly exclaiming: 'Who's available and has no ex-wife to get in the way? A widower!'

Widowers are rare and highly sought-after commodities. In the race for the perfect man, a widower is a good bet for a place or even a win. They have many things going for them: they're available, don't pay maintenance, and might even have ended up with a bit of an inheritance – life-assurance, an apartment, a house, etc. With a little luck, his children will be grown up, and with even more luck, Madame tip-toed off stage without a heart-rending story, no interminable chemotherapy, just one of those stupid things, sudden but not violent, that can happen to anyone at any time.

Be warned though, there is only a very narrow window for bagging a widower, between the slightly vague period when his mourning ends and his social resurrection. After that, it's too late, you can be sure he's already spoken for.

The brooding widower you're hoping to console is only weighed down by one thing you can't fight against: his memories. Initially, you'll have to put up with this. But once you're settled in, you need to subtly deconstruct the decorative influence of the absent woman, who's a bit too present for your liking. If by chance your new squeeze has left a mysterious urn in pride of place on the mantelpiece, you'll have to think about letting it go. But how? Moving a piece of furniture is easy, repainting the kitchen is doable, getting rid of a chandelier or a carpet he bought with Her in Iran isn't impossible. You can always put it on Gumtree and tell him one day it went for an amazing price. However, even at auction, even on eBay for a token price, the urn from the mantelpiece is going to be hard to offload. I can imagine the listing: 'Urn for sale, barely used, nearly new – 1 euro, shipping not included – sober, contemporary design, would suit any style. Offers accepted.' Having her disappear from his life for a second time without consultation isn't fair play, and neither is relegating her to the cellar.

The method for catching a widower in the period when his psychological and sexual fundamentals are reawakened will depend on his particular needs, which you'll have to grasp before anyone else. You'll have to decide if he prefers to be jollied along, or needs to take his time. It's up to you to cast your fine net into the river of possibilities and haul it in with no mishaps.

Of course, my remarks are only valid if the widower is in his fifties or perhaps the first third of his sixties. Widowers in their seventies or eighties are more plentiful, but less attractive for our purposes. We're talking about the perfect man for a young fifty-something, remember.

'So where do we find these widowers?' Laurence explained to me that she'd signed up to a group providing psychological support to people who'd lost a spouse. One day, she'd found out about this association that helps people through the mourning process and offered to take part in the support group. She hadn't lost anyone in the sense that the people around her understood it, and she didn't want to lie either, so she spoke about loss in general, without giving any specific details. Early on, she spoke up at a meeting to say that rather than wallowing in mournful feelings, she hoped to rediscover joy and life as soon as possible, and why not, she heard herself say, find a new companion. They all agreed and applauded her bravery. She went to a few meetings and spotted a brand-new widower who was kind and cute. One day, at the end of the session, she asked him out for a drink. They now live happily together, and already had lots of children.

A few weeks after my terrible tart party, I came across a wonderful widower. A good background, distinguished looks, an unusual job, a château in Normandy, polished and at ease on every level. I'll spare you the CV, which wouldn't fit in a tweet even though his prestigious university is identified by just one letter . . . From what I could see, the curtains of his window were slightly open. All I had to do was close one eye, open the other wide, find the right words, load the arrow and draw back the bow.

But he didn't seem to take much initiative. Was he interested? Was I interested if he wasn't? I'm a shy princess of the very old school, having been taught that the man makes the moves. So I did nothing. Of course, this strategy hasn't always been successful, as it's often the boldest who've claimed the prize, to the detriment of those who weren't decisive enough, but whom I might have liked more. Nevertheless, you don't change your losing ways at fifty. In any case, I'd rather die than take the first step. So I did the proper thing and waited patiently.

He invited me to spend New Year's Eve with him, and as I'm charitable, generous and naïve, I asked one of my pretty, single friends to join us. 'But why?' people asked me later. I can't answer that.

Over the course of the evening, I saw her perform several impeccable moves. Nothing was said or done by chance, her show was a work of art, a plan in two parts, perfection, seduction, grace. You couldn't blame her, but I was gloating in advance over the inevitable brick wall in front of her. In any case, that's what I told myself the next day when she called me to ask for his number so she could thank him. So imagine my surprise when I received a letter from her a few weeks later, inviting me to spend a weekend at the château and warmly thanking me for having introduced her to the man who was now sharing her life and making her so happy.

They're still together.

But really, to steal a widower . . .

What lesson should I learn from this episode? To wait or to strike? At this point in my story, I still wasn't sure if there was one correct answer.

It was to wait, of course.

The perfect man does not have a beard

There's a reason for the way men wear their facial hair. That it's become non-negotiable by this point is irritating, and not just to the cheeks. More than a fashion accessory, beards have now become the touchstone of the most endemic herd-following behaviour.

Beards project an image somewhere between virility and affectation, and for a long while I wondered what to think. I think I was waiting until I was sure of my judgement on the subject. After all, our opinions can change, sometimes radically. There was actually a time when I liked blond men with highlights and shoes with pompoms. Our backstories are filled with examples of poor taste that are merely passing phases. (And I won't even mention the men.)

Wearing a beard is one of those fashions that follow the whims of trendsetters, fashion designers, Art Directors, metropolitan hipsters, gays and yogi masters. Beards represent uniformity born out of boredom. For men over fifty, beards are only acceptable if they're not white, or even grey, which is problematic as these areas are the first to go. Otherwise, it's an absurdity. The same goes for dyeing it, and if that's what you're doing boys, you've gone through the looking glass. In the time it takes to grow a beard, I see dashing, funny fifty-somethings suddenly transform into hairy old ashtrays. Not to mention the state of our skin if the ashtray decides to try anything more than a kiss on the cheeks.

In the throes of passion, we have better things to do than protecting our chins with our hands.

So STOP IT, my dears!!

You think you look cool, but it just makes you look older!

That's enough now!

Have a nice close shave and come over here.

Now give us a kiss.

And let's have no more of it.

My perfect man shaves in the evening.

Is the perfect man less of a catch than you?

Calculate the equation based on age, beauty, height, social standing and bank account and you'll be able to guess which half of a couple is likely to dominate the relationship. Of course, this is all more of a question of statistics than mathematics. But basically, an old, ugly, broke guy will not normally have the upper hand and never will, unless he has some legendary horizontal skills confirmed by indiscreet beneficiaries. And even then, those qualities dry up over time. A younger, professionally successful partner will take permanent control, unless any family neuroses emerge, such as an adored or hated mother, which come down to the same thing on the scale of marital difficulties. Similarly, with the boot on the other foot, if I was a man, I would be extremely suspicious of women who adore or detest their fathers.

If you think that it's better to choose someone who's less of a catch than you to reduce the chances of him leaving you, then think again. We can rely on life to teach us that these men are not necessarily the safest option. Imagine the day when the man in question suddenly ups and leaves, even though you thought your contribution to the relationship was far superior to his. Your pride suffers a double blow: the break-up itself, and being left by a harmless loser. So always go for a notch above, even if it's only for a giggle, by which I mean someone younger, taller, and all the rest. Your friends will have renewed respect for you, and the next candidates will be of the same calibre.

For a long time, I roamed around, searching unobtrusively but in vain. It was no good, none of the free single men I came across had the basic qualities that simple girls like me are looking for: kindness, respect, manners, confidence. So many abortive attempts, near misses, dead ends, bad choices; men who were very married, too young, bruised or battered. But serious, stable, 'normal' guys, genuine possibilities: nothing, never, nobody. So I ended up making the following resolution: 'if you can't have a good one, have no one'.

A few bits of advice

Avoid married men

Now, of course, there's always the possibility of borrowing one of your friends' husbands with no plans to give him back. But that's stealing, and it's not acceptable. You'll lose your friend, of course, and the wrath of Olympus will come down on you. Bad karma!

Personally, I've never had a taste for married men apart from those who have been separated for years and settled all their business. A fling with a married man distributes pain before/after, which is what makes the 'during' interesting but it's a dangerous game and takes a heavy toll. At worst, a long love affair with a married man will lead you into self-hatred, at best, it will provide amusement, but only for so long. Men are cowards and will always prefer their comfort to managing complications or coming to terms with their feelings. It's patience that wins (or loses), and the impatient one who loses (or wins), and frankly, there are better things to do. On the supposition that guilt in high doses can ruin your health, let's not go there.

To avoid married men is simple, just ignore them.

They must remain surrounded by an impenetrable halo, so any penetration is strictly prohibited.

Beware the things that married men say, which are always the same:

He no longer makes love to his wife. **False.**

He's sure that his wife is cheating on him. **False.**

He never cheated on his wife before you came along. **False.**

He no longer gets on with his wife. **Partly false.**

He's planning to leave her. **False.**

And we can also add the following list:

He often cancels at the last minute. **True.**

For different reasons to the ones he gives you. **True.**

Be aware of the risk that your relationship with a married man could end the day his wife finds out. The ball will then be in your court.

Because once the truth is discovered, the husband banged to rights and the infidelity admitted, the wife's priority will be to keep her husband. The husband's priority will be to keep his mistress.

One of my friends who had succumbed to the practised seduction of a married man found herself saddled with the wrath of a wife who wanted to know, and one day found out. One evening, she took up residence on the landing outside my friend's apartment with machetes, knives and Kalashnikovs in her eyes.

When the mistress came home, she saw this woman sitting on the steps, with an expression that was clear enough to render introductions unnecessary.

'But what do you want? What are you doing here?' stammered my dumbstruck friend.

'If you come near my man one more time,' the wife replied, in a tone that invited no response, 'I'M GOING TO KILL YOU.'

Despite the intensity of the affair, the mistress decided that the stakes were too high. The relationship ended immediately.

Don't be the rebound girl

With a little luck, you'll be able to catch one on the fly just after his separation. That's all well and good, but be sure to leave a little time, so as not to be the rebound girl. She's the one who will pay dearly for the previous failure, and may well have the dubious pleasure of a difficult relationship that doesn't last. She won't see the wall she's heading towards at high speed. There always has to be one, so best leave it to someone else.

The way to play it is to be there at the right moment, ready to pounce, staking out like a sniper on the battlements of patience, in a heightened state of alert.

Look out for the losers

Be wary of a man who has never had a wife or any long-term relationships. A man who hasn't had any children, or has left more than one partner pole-axed. They're known, documented and you keep them at a distance, at best saying hello, but more than two sentences or one drink in their company is strictly forbidden. If you're in doubt, take a good look on Google, read between the lines, investigate his Instagram stories, ask the mutual friends you find on Facebook (if there are none, that's really weird), call the Duluc Detective Agency, or for want of a better solution, ask one of his exes to spill the beans: men always pick up and dump in the same way. At our age, we have no more time to waste on twisted guys, all the more so because there are a lot of them around.

So let's go straight to the good guys. Oh, you think all this lacks mystery? Well, yes, I know my dear, but I'm at an age where the years count triple, so I'm grateful for the warning. My fragile, impatient little heart thanks you in advance.

The eternal bachelor complains about his difficulty in falling in love, but can just as easily moan about falling in love too easily. And when he proclaims his hope that one day he will find true love, everyone sniggers. Meanwhile, he apologises to anyone who'll listen for his erratic emotional attitudes in the past, and the consequences that he can't deal with. Some of your friends will have paid the price in tears, despite having been warned.

Then there's the fashionable specimen who is being produced in industrial quantities these days: the perverse narcissist. One of the advantages of maturity is having already encountered someone like this, stumbled into his nets, known the fear he inspired and learnt how to identify others like him. A twisted relationship with a perverse narcissist is like chickenpox, you only get it once, and then the vaccine lasts a whole lifetime.

So why are there so many? Is it due to the cut-rate ego expansion provided by social media? Or the little prince tendency of upbringings dispensed by domineering mothers who create twisted adults? Whatever the reason, I urge you to pay particular attention to anyone who issues unjustified reproaches, cuts you off mid-sentence, pays excessive compliments to pretty girls in your presence, or makes insistent references to his exes, who were so wonderful . . . Any of this behaviour is a good reason to run a mile. Because if you refuse to submit, a perverse narcissist can become dangerous: endless repetition, victimisation, lies, insincerity, accusations, harassment . . . Nothing is his fault. He destroys his partner's personality over time. As a manipulator, he takes advantage of 'friends' who are always temporary. He never holds on to people. Like any good predator, he is only out for his own interests, and relishes the destruction of others. A perverse narcissist is a virus, and a virus needs to be eradicated. They can just as easily be women as men.

These days, the paradoxical effect of the popularity of this specimen encourages every woman with a relationship on the skids to see her future ex as the epitome of a perverse narcissist. According to one of my lawyer friends who specialises in family cases, one in every two women comes to her office armed with pages photocopied from a specialist book on the subject. They brandish them furiously as justification for demanding an increase in their maintenance payments.

All the same, we should beware the crazy desire to 'meet someone at all costs', which can encourage us to forgive these charming men some unpalatable things. We're so keen for it to work that our common sense takes a dip at the approach of any kind of possible partner.

I remember a charming man whose prospectus fulfilled pretty much all of my criteria: available, boss of his own company, good looking, younger than me but not too much, a child living with his ex, a willing appendage with a nice feel to it . . . Anyway, I'd decided to overlook the cultural dimension of art and literature, which was a fairly weak area. But perfection doesn't exist, I told myself as if to excuse him for his crass ignorance. Wanting it to work so badly, I'd persuaded myself in cases like this that complementarity was the key to relationship success, whereas similar profiles meant boredom was inevitable. Thanks to this slightly idiotic conviction that you have to be different to get along, I've found myself dating some very unusual men. Sometimes too unusual.

One day, we were in the car on our way to someone's house for dinner. I was driving, as he'd been banned for a year. I hate driving in two situations: at night, because I can't see properly, and with a man who sits beside me in silence with his foot tensed over an imaginary brake pedal. The fact that he was commenting on my driving didn't help me relax. He started off with advice ('Why not try the left-hand lane?'), then ironic remarks ('Have you really passed your test?'), orders ('Go back down to second'), before moving on to increasingly aggressive and judgemental commands. I imagined a man squeezing the trigger as he looked at me through his sights. The volume went up, the tempo as well, and the words of my handsome new soon-to-be-ex lover began to resemble insults. I realised that he was crazy. But a bit of my brain was in denial and continued to resist. It took a few more unacceptable humiliations before I resolved to leave him.

Beware the super-fit

You should also be suspicious of men in their fifties with 'bodies to die for': rippling stomachs, buttocks worthy of a Greek sculpture, bulging muscles, chiselled pectorals and a torso brandishing a V for victory over the passing years. What a trauma! The motivation of these body-obsessed fitness fanatics is overwhelming narcissism rather than taking good care of themselves. Dig a little deeper and you'll discover they load themselves up with seeds, seaweed and protein twenty minutes after their exertions. And if you discover a tub of creatine in a drawer, once again, the only solution is a sharp exit.

Assiduously keeping in shape, yes, relentless fixation, help.

The consequences of being in love

Remember the extent to which being in love influenced our behaviour in the past, sometimes even making us do ridiculous things? How many risks have we taken in the name of love? Nowadays, we're less impulsive and more reasonable under the influence of this marvellous emotion than in our younger years. We keep our feet on the ground and our heads on our shoulders because we know through experience that the slightest miscalculation can have us sliding down the mountain on our backsides. You slide quicker at fifty.

The collateral damage and side-effects are numerous, particularly at the beginning and end of a relationship. On the minus side, there's disordered eating, loss of concentration, a slump in turnover, uncontained frustration and a windmill constantly whirring in your head. On the plus side: sudden weight loss, sweet reveries, a surge in libido, oxytocin at fever pitch, a permanent feeling of floatation and once again that windmill constantly whirring in your head ... We take off the brake and let ourselves go, without knowing if the slope goes up or down.

Yet fundamentally, the idea of love and the state of being in love are things that have nothing to do with what women in their fifties are looking for, in other words a lasting, loving relationship based on shared feelings and quality time. A good piece of advice but not one that's always easy to follow is to ensure you don't fall in love with someone who doesn't love you. If he doesn't love you, he's not worthy of your love.

One of my friends was deeply in love with a man who'd stopped loving her. One day, she confided in me that he'd told her: 'I've had enough of your love.' I sometimes wonder how some of us get over these things.

But if everything is mutual – love, the idea of the love, the effects of love and the understanding it brings – then let's go for it.

Eyes closed. Eyes open. Enjoying the thrills.

Let's abandon ourselves to this great mixture of the three stages of love that we crave without knowing it at this stage of our lives: a touch of Eros, a few drops of Philia and a good slice of Agape.

So should we be wary about being in love? Yes, a little, but we should still seek it out, without losing heart.

And maybe find it?

Yes, but when?

The meter's running!

Don't be too picky

'I've had enough,' Elisa complained, 'I never meet anyone!'

'But are you looking in the right place, are you spotting the right ones?' I replied.

Elisa is a very beautiful young fifty-something, an ex-model who's been spoilt in the past, is accustomed to respect and has an eye for appearance and fine fabrics. She was depressed about not being able to find a man to share her life. At first, I struggled to understand. She's so sweet and pretty that if there was one fifty-something in the world I wasn't worried about, it was her. But a while ago, she told me about her umpteenth romantic failure, which set me thinking.

'So I met a man I liked. Fifty-four, physically not bad at all, bags of charm, not uninteresting. He told me about his divorce, his children, his collection of old books, his organic vegetable garden, his flying club (yes, he goes gliding), his experience as a volunteer in a refugee camp, his thesis on Georges Bataille*, the latest app he's built that Google wants to buy . . . The other day, he offered to take me away for the weekend. I agreed, and he took me to his house of the Île d'Oléron, which is a lovely old place.'

'He sounds great, this guy. So what happened next?'

'In the evening, we were due to go for dinner with some friends, and he appears, you won't believe this, in a pair of Geox shoes and a short-sleeved checked shirt!'

'Yes well, that's not too bad. It's a detail.'

'A detail? Are you kidding? An important detail! Naturally, I explained to him that he couldn't carry on wearing things like that. And he told me, "My friends don't care." So I replied, "Perhaps your friends don't,

---

* Translator's note: influential and provocative French novelist, poet and essayist.

but I do." Well, do you know what? He said I was too bossy! These men, you try to sort them out, to help them improve, but they're not happy. Well, you know what? He can keep his checked shirt and his breathable shoes!'

It seems to me that Elisa is trapped in a syndrome of perfection, which inevitably leads to failure. Finding someone right for her would demand too much involvement, be too difficult to manage, be too nice. The fear of failure leads her to conspire with destiny. She looks for the thing about the other person that isn't right, that she can't accept, and she finds it, making any connection impossible, let alone building any kind of relationship. For Elisa, no one will ever be elegant enough. Even before she gets to know them, they're already guilty of poor taste.

I could happily have suggested she see a therapist.

But of course, I'd forgotten, she is a therapist.

Don't take the plunge before you're ready

Two thousand years ago, Marie-Ange was in class 6B with me. Life took its course: marriage, then two children who grew up and left home. One day, years later, I met up with her again: blonde, tanned and freshly separated from her unfaithful husband, who'd suddenly upped and left her after thirty-three years together.

How would she recover from this sudden departure? Some say it takes double the time you spent with someone to rebuild yourself. So in sixty-six short years, Marie would be out of the woods. But that would be a bit late, night would have fallen. I advised her to find someone new as soon as possible. In principle, she agreed, but for the moment, she needed to find her identity. She had never worked, and clung on to the idea of a perfect family, so much so that she forgot herself. Now that everything had collapsed, she didn't know where to begin. And yet she said she was ready for a new relationship. So I said I'd help her write her profile for a dating site that some of my friends had singled out for the quality of its visitors.

A little while later, Marie-Ange was transformed: a new look, a new haircut, a new life. She'd moved into town, to a magnificent apartment with a panoramic terrace.

'I'm doing something I'd never done before in my life,' she told me, 'I'm working. I'm selling cakes, ice creams, chocolates. I get to meet people. I have a social life. I'm no longer ashamed of going to a bar or a restaurant on my own. In the evenings I read, mainly personal development books, or I watch series. I'm rediscovering my true self.'

'Wonderful! And what about the dating site, any results?'

'Absolutely nothing. All disasters. Lots of the men

I meet have one thing on their minds: if they're not looking for easy sex, they want a roof over their heads. Most of them are divorced, their wives have kept the house, and they'd like to move out of their bedsits. I can see them coming. When they say, "Nice place you've got here", I can tell they're ready to turn up with a suitcase.'

She couldn't stand the idea of someone taking advantage of her, of being used by a squatter and robbed of her time. After the trauma of her husband's sudden departure, Marie-Ange first needs to rebuild herself before she can trust again – trust herself at first, and then another man after that. It'll take time, but I'm sure that once she's recovered, dealt with her anger and finalised her divorce, she'll meet someone. She doesn't know it yet, but he'll be the right one.

In the land of the therapists and fortune-tellers

When everything is unstable, what or who can you cling to? Besides the cat and your friends, there is a whole range of options of varying degrees of reliability and effectiveness.

How to find a therapist discreetly

The period when I was assiduously looking for a man to share my life with was when I was at my lowest ebb. I was constantly unbalanced, everything was my fault, I was hopeless, useless, losing the plot. I looked at other people. Why was I broken down by the side of the road? If my friends and coaches couldn't find the right words, who would?

That was when I had a thought that occurs to many of us at some point: what if I went to see 'someone', as they say? Someone to help me see clearly. After all, there's no shame in it. But who? I couldn't see myself asking my friends: 'Do you know a good shrink?'

'Why's that, is something the matter?'

No chance. With the help of the internet, I would find a discreet solution. There were several in the neighbourhood, the closest being exactly 267 metres away. Rather than choosing on the basis of style, school or type, I decided to rely on geolocation, a decision with as much logic to it as there is mathematical reasoning in a tombola.

'How did you find me?' asked Dr X at our first appointment.

'In the yellow pages.'

Not a good start. I could sense her irritation at the lack of a recommendation.

At two sessions a week, my monthly expenditure on therapy, non-deductible and with no guarantee of results, helped to take my living standards down by two notches. But for the best possible cause, namely my mental state. It's absurd to spend that much money on crying in front of a stranger, isn't it? But then again, isn't it preferable to open up your personal rubbish chute in front of someone you're paying to listen rather than boring your friends by pouring it all out in front of them?

My therapist would smile at my jokes. Sometimes, she would burst out laughing at the comical situations that I tried hard to describe with as much humour as possible, and even ask for more. To the point that I sometimes wondered who should be paying whom. Once, I even managed to make her laugh and cry during the same session. The first part of the session had consisted of one of the exercises used in her particular brand of therapy. The sort that specialists in Cognitive Behavioural Therapy give to their patients, like listing their qualities, asking their close friends to do the same, recounting an enjoyable moment in their week, describing their negative emotions, complimenting themselves out loud, and so on. That day, to boost my self-confidence, my therapist wanted to teach me to say NO.

THERAPIST Go on, ask me a question, I'll show you how to stand firm.

ME OK then. You're too expensive and I don't want to keep on paying your exorbitant fees, which I can't claim back from the health authorities. It's ridiculous and I can't afford it. I'm asking you for a reduction due to the distress your fees are causing me. They're so high they make my sessions ineffective.

THERAPIST No, that's not possible. These are my normal fees that I charge everyone. I have overheads, the rent, taxes to pay . . .

I carried on arguing but she just laughed and wouldn't back down. The session then continued on a more serious note. We moved on to a second exercise, and I started reading the description of myself I'd jotted down the day before on the back of an envelope. My task was to paint a portrait of myself, in essence to answer the question 'Who am I?'. I wrote about my childhood, my teenage stammer and the way people made fun of it, cruel heartbreaks, my dysfunctional family. Then there was the excessive focus on emotions, how I grew up, with a lot of stuff about my father, who was already at the centre of everything I'd mentioned before. The text stopped suddenly as the handwriting became jittery and broke down, betraying the rage and tears that led to a broken pencil lead. When I finished reading, I looked up. My therapist sniffed, grabbed a handy tissue and dried her eyes.

'You make me cry,' she said, apologising. 'That's the end of the session for today.'

Her tears knocked me off balance for a few seconds, because I assumed she must have heard much worse secrets than mine. I wouldn't wish my father on anyone, but all the same, he's not a torturer, he never assaulted me or locked me in a cellar. My final conclusion was that she's a very sensitive soul. It's true that because therapists set themselves up as the gatekeepers of our diagnosis, we tend to expect them, coldly, to provide the key to our problems, the therapeutic solution to our anxieties. We share our most secret hopes with them and expect a rapid improvement, or failing that, at least a better understanding of ourselves. Seeing my therapist's weakness made her more human, but her emotion was encroaching on my personal territory, and that felt strange. Could she really give me what I was expecting from her? Because all I was interested in was meeting the man of my life.

How to leave your therapist

From their hold over our emotions to the financial manna that we represent, therapists do not want to hear us say 'it's over'. But between you and me, who does? Whilst they're teaching us how to say no, one day we find ourselves telling them in a roundabout way that we've met someone, and don't need them anymore. Because that's the truth of it, after all. 'But no, that's got nothing to do with it,' she says. Are you joking? It's got everything to do with it!

Depending on our ability to stand up to them, we'll take timid steps forward, or disappear suddenly. The only effective technique, which is also valid for an unsatisfactory relationship, is to cut it off in one go, thwack, straight through, a clean break: 'Hold it! I'm telling you that I won't be coming back!'

Because you see, when you want to stop your psychotherapy, shaky conviction is unproductive. It's difficult to meet the gaze of someone who gained a sort of power over you the day he or she offered you the box of tissues. Someone who has smugly and shrewdly dealt with the classic transference process, keeping you at a distance when you were dreaming of sleeping with him (if it was a him) or becoming her best friend (if it was a her).

But one day, you take the plunge and get straight to the point. 'I'm stopping . . . [pause]. Yes, I've decided to stop.' Not only does the therapist not move, you're forced to repeat yourself: 'Yes, I'm stopping . . . I'm going to stop, I've realised I don't need this anymore. My head's in a good place, so I can do without our sessions.' At this point, a one-ton silence bears down on the couch. You worry the response will be an aggressive 'You're joking, I hope.' For a few seconds, you struggle for breath, sorry you didn't take the slightly crooked approach of using phoney excuses about your availability or your financial problems, or didn't think to say (slightly spinelessly), 'I'll have to call you to confirm the appointment,' which, naturally, you'd never have done. But standing firm, looking your shrink in the eye and saying 'this is our last session' is an act of courage that demands respect. Be prepared for the usual response: 'OK, we'll talk about it next week.' (True story.)

Once, at a dinner, I met a film-maker who shall remain nameless but admitted to seeing a psychotherapist for twenty-five years. 'The first two years were marvellous, and then I spent twenty-three years trying to stop.' After this revelation, he immediately fell asleep, just like that, sitting there at the dinner table, with his chin on his chest, and the guests all around continuing their conversation as if nothing had happened. After ten minutes, he started to snore. I know the two things are entirely unconnected, but I can't help thinking that his therapist must have become a crutch, and that this was linked to his state of relaxation.

In my case, the day that I pulled myself together, regaining my autonomy and a certain equilibrium, I announced at the end of a session that I was going to stop. Caught off-guard, my therapist was dumbstruck, but fought back. 'No!' she said. 'You can't just stop like that, overnight. These appointments are no laughing matter, after all.' She was right. A hundred euros, twice a week, for a forty-minute session was no laughing matter. Above all, I'd realised I had become obsessed by the idea of making her happy. I did everything I could to interest her, distract her or make her laugh. Every time, I left her office exhausted by my own verbal diarrhoea. So of course, when she told me that we would need three sessions a week to manage my neuroses, I thought I could take advantage to save some energy. It was a real struggle, but I managed it. However, she did provide me with two or three inspiring little phrases that were really helpful and have stuck with me to this day.

Should you visit a fortune-teller?

In September, when she'd just turned thirty-eight and being single and on the hunt was starting to wear a bit thin, my niece Caroline went to see a fortune-teller, who told her that she would meet her soulmate before the end of the year, get married soon after and have children, would you believe it? She lost no time in sharing this divine revelation with her friends – a group of smart, single bankers with no kids from the Trocadéro district. Some of them raised their eyes in disbelief, others merely wondered whether the fortune-teller hadn't laid it on a bit thick by including every one of the expected clichés.

Of course, when Caroline announced her marriage a fortnight after falling head over heels for a handsome young graduate from a top university who'd just sold his company, the fortune-teller's switchboard was inundated, and her diary filled up in the space of a few hours. One after the other, my cousin's friends visited her boudoir with their lists of questions that had nothing to do with the prospects for market-linked investments. Convinced that the fortune-teller had the power to align the planets, they all wanted to know when they would finally meet the handsome, rich, unattached prince charming they'd been waiting for.

Her name and number were surreptitiously passed around. And guess who managed to get her hands on them?

When you arrive at the fortune-teller's house in Boulogne, it's all red velvet like in the movies, with carved elephant's tusks and African masks. It could all put the fear of God into you if the lady, a slightly hippyish woman in her sixties, didn't immediately kiss you on the cheeks before asking, 'Would you like a drink, love?' to put you at your ease. She told me that one day a slightly constipated air-conditioned banking type flinched at her embrace. 'But we don't know each other,' she said. 'You can't call me love and kiss me like that.' I laughed, because I might have thought the same thing if I wasn't so shy – on paper, I'm bold as brass, but face to face, I'm not so full of myself. The fortune-teller had shown her the door, yelling at her to 'Get out' with enough brutality to invite no arguments. So it was with a half tense, half relaxed smile that I spread out the cards on the table as she'd asked.

First, she saw a woman, someone close to me who had it in for me. A toxic blonde, she added: 'Ooh, a real nasty piece of work. She lives on the ground floor. Is it the concierge?' Then threw a card down on to mine and shouted, 'F**k her!'

I sat there petrified, not moving, not saying anything. I thought I'd identified the ground-floor blonde, a courtesan passing herself off as a businesswoman, and quite skilled in the art of raising funds for personal use. Numerous victims had suffered at her hands, one of whom had warned me just before I went into business with her.

'Go on then, lay your next cards on top of these four. Well, this is all very good, you're travelling, you're writing and you're going to be published!'

At the time, I still hadn't planned to write a book or been approached by a publisher. I should have jumped for joy. WHAT? I'm going to write a book and be published? But when? And what about? Instead, I immediately asked:

'But am I going to meet someone?'

'Put one down there, there and there. Hmm, I don't see you alone, no you're not alone. He's not far away, there's a lot of love between you, lots of gentleness, I see you living together.'

'When?'

'Now listen, don't start, this isn't an exact science!'

Then she moved on from my future to her past, giving me her potted history, digressing and getting bogged down in stories, returned to my love life, got side-tracked talking about a famous ex-lover (me: 'No! What him? . . . Wow!'). But I wasn't listening any more, I didn't want any more details, she'd told me what I wanted to hear.

At the end, I got up.

'How much do I owe you?'

'It's up to you.'

I thought of my niece, who couldn't have given enough after her prediction of marriage and happiness, so to compensate, I didn't hold back . . . If she'd asked for the amount I gave her, it would have seemed incredibly expensive, but given the good news, I felt I was getting an amazing bargain.

So should you visit a fortune-teller? I don't know, but should you visit that one? Unequivocally yes. Afterwards, I felt like I'd had a massage at the Ritz on Prozac. I left her house so happy that once I was back on the street, I jumped in the air and went on my way dancing. Then I stopped, confused. OK, I'm going to meet someone. But when? And where? And how will I find him?

How to find a (fifty-year-old) man at fifty

On a dating site

O genie of the lamp, let a global computer bug wipe out my online dating history.

There's nothing on the horizon, and the few men you

do meet are all unsuitable in one way or another. But where are the others hiding? You've ventured beyond the familiar concentric circles, but still come up empty-handed.

So in complete secrecy, you take the plunge.

Even though when friends had suggested it, you replied loud and clear: 'Oh no, never, it's not for me,' and until the year before, it would have been out of the question. Back then, you'd almost been tempted to make fun of those who'd gone down that route. You thought there was singular lack of romance, unexpectedness or magic to meeting your man on the internet.

And then finally, in the dim light of the screen in which anything goes, and at the insistence of a friend who was tired of hearing about your bad dates and having to arrange dinner parties with odd numbers, you finally decide to register with that allegedly exclusive site for discriminating singles. 'Promise you'll spill the beans,' the friend insists. People sitting comfortably like nothing better than a bit of vicarious excitement. 'I promise,' you reply, determined to tell her as little as possible.

You only tacitly acknowledge your fear of coming across people you know online, like the local resident single guy, for example, or your neighbour across the landing, both of whom fish for most of their prey on the internet. But this is nothing to the fear of coming across one of your friends' boyfriends. It's better not to know, so you don't have to say anything to your infatuated friend when she's wondering if there's a legitimate reason for her heartache.

After you've chosen your requirements regarding age, height and level of education, a candidate appears on the screen. Like you, he's made the effort to come up with some nice turns of phrase to create a really flattering image with his profile. To be sure that the search engine catches you in its net, you've both cheated a tiny bit, him about his height, you about your age, telling yourself that if the relationship goes anywhere you'll wipe away this post-truth with a click. You've put his CQ (Cultural Quotient) under the microscope by studying his favourite films, books and artists. You were delighted to discover you both have the same level of education, and share a passion for hiking and various other peripheral interests that you imagined would make perfect ice-breakers.

Experience shows that to move on to the oral, you have to take care with your written work, choose good talking points, as the politicians say, and watch out for the nutters, as I say. Being the recipient of crushes, likes and hearts feels good, but don't forget to be wary.

For a single young fifty-something, sex is an unpredictable, disruptive experience, leaving you always on edge. To be or not to be in sync, that is the question.

And it's impossible to know if it will be a winning match or a dead loss, without at least having played a part of it. From the first time, your partner will try to deliver a performance honed to the best of his abilities, but good or bad, the first impression is fundamental.

The problem with virtual contact is that sexual compatibility can't be described on a dating site profile, only discovered thanks to a shot in the dark that will decide whether the candidate will be called back for another chance in the second week. The bodily choreography that occurs when we're physically attracted to someone is never spontaneous when you're selecting someone on the basis of photographic or written criteria. It's hard to trigger desire by just reading a profile, you'll need courage, practice and precautions, all of which dampen the enthusiasm. You also need to concentrate, in order to be more efficient, without letting yourself be distracted by details linked to the discovery of the other person: his skin, his breathing, the sounds he makes. Make do with the constraints and content yourself with the results. Get to the bottom of things.

I've never had a relationship with a man I've met on a dating site, but have had countless 'drinks' with so-called possibilities. These men generally had a specific goal in mind that they wanted to achieve quickly, and as I like to take things slow, we were never able to seal the deal.

A dating site, with its profusion of slightly lost people in search of a pleasant surprise, is a place full of loneliness, distress, disappointment and deceit. You move around like a pilot fish, glass in hand like at a cocktail party, say hello or good evening, and when you spend some time on someone, you can't help thinking that you could find an even better man, if you took a bit more trouble and stayed a little longer. And at the same time, that's exactly what the other person is thinking. Visiting a site is a process based on dissatisfaction, reward, punishment and addiction, a bit like a casino. Rejection becomes normal. You get hurt and get used to it. You reveal your least respectable tastes. In short, it's not for everyone.

Let loose into this bayou of predators, the single young fifty-something will struggle at first with the rules of love 3.0, which generate flat-pack feelings: fleeting, intense and soluble. She wasn't prepared for this new market but will learn fast. If she uses it intelligently she'll be able to find pleasure and perhaps even a good man.

PS: To some of my friends, who will know who they are: don't try to make out you met him at a dinner in town hosted by 'people you don't know', a private view or a motorway services.

Not to me.

Don't worry, I won't tell anyone, I promise, and I'll pretend to believe you.

Thirty-somethings are comfortable with meeting their soulmate on the internet, and even find it funny to have the mayor mention it in his speech at the town hall ceremony. But we fifty-somethings raised on a classical education and romantic novels are a little embarrassed by the results, speed and effectiveness of this approach. Taking things slowly has its charm.

And when you give up . . .

As I had no man in my life, there was nothing and no one around me, and the only man I liked didn't want me, well, too bad, enough was enough. So I solemnly decided to do without. I wasn't going to 'sell myself cheap' simply to be with someone. The fortune-teller's prediction had left me a little hope, of course, but frankly, after several months of travelling, loneliness and abstinence, I said to myself that it was all nonsense. I wondered if I was too old to meet someone. Would I ever make love again? And if I did, would I be able to enjoy it again? In any case, I accepted the idea of giving up. I welcomed in my emotional solitude, handed it a permanent contract and decided to live with it.

Or without it, strictly speaking. In any case, I've notice a growing trend amongst single women these days of joyfully accepting the fact of being on their own, without a partner, at ease with their freedom and enjoying it to the full, and not even looking for anyone. They genuinely appreciate their solitude, their independence or their emotional and sexual eclecticism. These women don't think for a second about changing their way of life. They're not waiting for a man to fulfil a goal of settling down, they're self-sufficient. They're not planning to share their existence or their rent. So when I say that everyone's looking for love, yes perhaps. But is everyone looking for a man? Certainly not.

In any case, I'd made my decision, I would be like these women . . . on trend.

And of course it was at the point when I gave up that the stars aligned, two by two, in my sky.

There they are.

I can see them.

During those years, I saw the Disastrous Man, but not often, because even from a distance, his beauty was watching. We still had a nice understanding, and after four years, we could say that we'd become friends. I'd always pretended not to have been affected by my terrible 'night of the tarts', and we never spoke about it. Then by chance, I heard from someone else that his relationship with the girl down south had sprung a leak. I didn't know the details, but 'Go for it!' was the advice from one of my friends.

'No, certainly not.' I didn't want to be the rebound girl between Miss Cote d'Azur and another thirty-something. He kept quiet about his emotional difficulties, but I noticed he became more receptive to me.

I pretended not to notice anything.

I wasn't interested.

So when he tried to kiss me at the end of a dinner, I turned my head, stood firm and said: 'No, let's not spoil everything. Let's stay friends.'

A week later, we saw each other again, and he told me clearly that he wanted to be with me, that he was sure of it. Wrapped in my paper pride, I refused again. No, really no, honestly! Then he struck a match, brought it very close and kissed me. I cracked and transformed into a candle, into liquid, burning, melting, flowing. I was flooded with an enormous sense of fear coupled with a dark desire. If I give in, this man will devastate me. My heart's airbags exploded in my chest, the security alarms put in place by fifteen years of single life screamed:

NO, NO, NO.

'OK,' I finally replied, but regretted it immediately because it was the day before I was flying to the US, and I was planning to stay for a month. He joined me there a week later. Our relationship began precisely at the moment we met up on an avenue in the East Village.

'But why didn't you make a move earlier? When I was four years younger!'

His answer was something like 'I couldn't see, I wasn't ready', and for a long time I went with that. It was only later, over time, as I got to know his complex programming, that I understood. But that's another story.

I remember saying to my friend Christine that I'd met a man I was very much in love with and vice versa. We were eating at Le Colonial, a restaurant on 57th Street in New York. She called the waiter over and asked for champagne, and then as if announcing a piece of good news, raised a toast: 'To the end of the hunt!'

Did the pairs of planets have to be standing to attention and incredibly well aligned for them to put the perfect incarnation of everything I loved in my path, at the time in my life when they say it's hardest to meet your soulmate?

After fifteen years of living alone, years of bad experiences and resigned solitude, it was with infinite happiness that I welcomed into my heart the gentle man whose axe had broken through its brand-new armour.

I'd finally found him.

My tall, bald, wonderful man. So sweet and gentle that it became my nickname for him: Le Doux!

The one the fortune-teller had been talking about.

I was no longer alone, I was now a couple! Oh yes! I'd have to learn to switch from 'I' to 'we'. No, *we* can't come on Sunday, *we* are having a weekend in the country. *We* are going to Cadaqués this summer.

I would have to fit new words into my everyday vocabulary: my love, my heart. New habits: 'How would you like to . . .?' Yes, I'd like to, yes to EVERYTHING. I was levitating. I had a permanent fixed grin inside. I must have made a strange impression.

The Young Fifty-Something
in a Relationship

'The older I get, the more I think that you can only live with people who set you free, who love you with an affection that weighs as lightly on you as it is powerful to feel. Life is too hard, too bitter for us to suffer yet more servitude at the hands of our loved ones'

Letter from Albert Camus to René Char

When love comes calling . . .

The unexpected arrival of love leaves us disorientated, unbalanced, thunderstruck. To either side of the wire we're still inexorably moving along lies the precipice with its possible devastation. The balancing bar in our hands stabilises. But only a little.

We know in advance that it won't be easy, we're not fools and we know all too well how the song goes, but we're so happy to finally be able to have another try, to abandon ourselves to feelings that we'd ended up believing were the preserve of youth.

Maintaining the state of love and ensuring it lasts as long as possible requires a minimum of strategy or maturity. It's dealing with what comes next that deserves our attention. Do you remember the days when we fell in love easily and our hearts did what they wanted? The strength of our emotions and the way they made all the decisions? How our minds were elsewhere in the office or in town, how it distracted us from our poor children and we spent double our salaries on lingerie or fripperies? Love became imperious, expanding its territory to the limits of the everyday and taking control of our bodies.

I like this brand-new love, and don't intend to watch it crumble. I want to keep it, observe it, preserve it and give it the benefit of what life has taught me.

Never show off

If you happen to have already met the perfect man who loves you and is sharing your life, button your lip, *s'il vous plaît*! There's nothing worse than happy people who want you to know about it. Happiness is based on intimate, infinitely subtle ingredients; it can dissolve at any moment, crushed by routine, indifference or a bad pun.

At the beginning, you want to shout your happiness from the rooftops, there are so many opportunities. But if later on, if your amorous exaltation starts to wane, and lethargy takes over, will you still be as keen to shout about it? To be madly in love for the first three years is easy. Beyond that it takes commitment, skill and two to tango. So, happy people, keep quiet from day one.

And if you cross paths with someone who knew you on the highway of your single days, who's going through the season of rejections, and he or she asks you how you're doing, tell them 'not bad' without sounding too enthusiastic. Keep the descriptions of your good fortune to yourself. And if it's a woman who's been on her own for a long time, be nice and add something like 'it must be tough' or 'I know the feeling.'

Learning to live with someone again

Getting used to living with someone again in your fifties isn't easy, especially on the back of fifteen years
of chronic singledom. We each have our set of non-
negotiables. Whereas we were all flexibility twenty years
ago, we've now stiffened up at the edges. Not to mention
our financial situations or the number of dependent
children, which are rarely symmetrical at the point when
the idea of living together surfaces. How much ground
will we be able to give? It's no problem accepting what we
already know, but how will we react to what we discover?

'Who moves in together at our age?' I've heard people
say. To which the answer was 'no one'. Of course, we all
know couples who got it together sometime around their
forties. But after fifty, take a good look . . .

It's a young people's thing, deciding to share the
same apartment, the same washing machine, the same
toothbrush mug. Habits can't just be changed. The decision to move in together 'late in the day' hinges on the
subtle combination of love, good economic sense and
spatial and temporal compatibility. The first two points
are known quantities when you make the decision, but
can potentially change. As for the third, only experience
will show how one person reacts in contact with the

other. An inch-perfect organisation of multiple rituals will gradually develop.

Le Doux and I already knew each other well, because we'd become friends. When we switched to 'love' mode, there was never really much hanging around. Which is fair enough, as it had gone on long enough . . . We moved into the first apartment we visited and happily merged our respective libraries, delighted at any duplicates. In his suitcase, he had a past life, children of various ages and two or three quirks that had to be accommodated: news on a drip feed, living and breathing music, a baby grand in the living room and the constant presence of laundry drying somewhere in the apartment (Le Doux disapproves of tumble dryers).

I adore the invasive, majestic presence of his baby grand, but struggle a bit more with the airer the size of half a Twingo in the hall covered with drying shirts and socks. My environmental credentials can't compete with the aesthetics of my living space, and I don't think the energy saving argument applies to apartment buildings designed to Baron Haussmann's standards. But that's the way it is, and as long as we're in love, I'll keep my views to myself.

I also had to explain to Pouppy that someone else had taken over, and I was less in need of his love. At this point, I remembered that my elderly parents, who were always wanting something, always ready with a quick reproach and in need of affection, liked to think of themselves as dyed in the wool cat-haters. Given that they're full of contradictions and have always said the opposite of what they thought, I suggested they could take Pouppy off my hands. They refused vehemently, which I took to mean yes, or even pretty please. I had to admit I was repeating my daughter's strategy. Like mother like daughter, or 'dogs don't give birth to cats', as we say in France. Since then, Pouppy has been enjoying himself in the south of France, where he receives the odd quick reproach and a lot of attention from my old dad.

Daily life: who does what under the same roof?

I've noticed that tasks are allotted according to an unspoken contract drawn up in the first few weeks. If you do the same thing several times in succession, it becomes your job. Are you in the habit of making the bed? You become responsible for the bed. Does he wash the pots? That's it, he always will. The tempo determined in the early days of the relationship will become set in stone.

It's fascinating to see how an affectionate gesture born out of love (or a trivial action dictated by mere circumstances), merely by being repeated twice, becomes a habit that itself develops into a function that makes the organ. So you become the organ that takes the rubbish out, makes the vinaigrette or washes the pan after you've had spaghetti. It's a disadvantage for those who want to do nothing, but with a little luck, you'll be able to share the tasks without having to make requests.

Active thirty-somethings will fall into the trap of the infamous 'mental load'*. A young fifty-something is no longer wet behind the ears, so she knows the ropes and should anticipate, determine a fair division and operate without prior negotiations. In the event of any doubt, you can discuss the subject openly, but informally and tactfully.

In my younger days, I remember not having been particularly enthralled by living at close quarters with a man, and always feeling disconcerted if he didn't keep his distance in the bathroom. As someone who hides away to clean my teeth and prides myself on being a pure spirit when it comes to bodily functions, I'm surprised to find myself transformed when my heart is full of love. I'm almost at the point of finding things that were

---

* Translator's note: although it does appear in English, this concept is much more common in French. It refers to the tendency to see the home as a woman's domain, so that even if chores are shared, women bear the 'mental load' of worrying about and managing domestic tasks.

once intolerable touching: noisy noses, digestive issues, repetitions . . . At any rate, I'm not bothered by all kinds of things that I pretend not to notice. At most, with the delicacy that comes with being in love, one of you will remark that something 'smells strange', so as to avoid the direct accusation of a forgetful sphincter having failed in its muscular vigilance.

Le Doux, meanwhile, helps to encourage this extreme indulgence. He's an easy man (to live with, I mean) with generally good manners, even though he spends hours reading in a place not originally designed for that purpose – like lots of men and very few women. It remains a mystery that the male colon should need literature whereas the pure female spirit is more likely to require a glycerine suppository. I can't help thinking of all the books I could have read if I'd taken my time and killed two birds with one stone.

Celebrate love, always

Valentine's Day is faithfully wheeled out year after year by the media and the advertising world, but this annual event leaves me perplexed. I'm told it would be nice for me to receive a bouquet of flowers or a heart-shaped cake on 14 February, but it seems to me that this Pavlovian response is unnecessary for those who say I love you and prove it every day.

Because if reciprocated feelings seem to go without saying for both parties, there's no need to mark the big day with daisies, going down on one knee and a Bulgari ring in a velvet box. Drawing a quick heart in the potato purée and then licking your finger with a suggestive look will do the trick. It will also leave your respective piggy banks intact, less than two months after taking a beating over the Christmas holidays. And then if your birthday, or your new lover's birthday, falls sometime around Christmas, things are going to mount up. So yes to nice little gestures, no to obligations.

And if you're single, all the Valentine's Day marketing simply trumpets the fact that you're still on your own. It's a celebration that leads to one of the most guilt-inducing social cruelties: 'Oh, so you haven't got anyone special? I'm so sorry!' In any case, there's nothing to stop you sending yourself a bouquet of roses with a note to explain the depth of your feelings, along the lines of 'if you want something done right, you're better off doing it yourself.'

If you are in a relationship, you can have a normal meal at home, with a bottle of Saint-Amour, for example, and a red rose in a single-stem vase, just to mark the occasion. And then you never know what you might find hidden in the potato purée . . . with a bit of luck, perhaps a Bulgari ring.

I sensed Le Doux's relief the day I told him I wasn't 'particularly interested' in jewellery. He read this passage with a forced smile on his face. I'm joking, My Love . . . I adore potato purée.

Jealousy

How to fight jealousy

A third of men are unfaithful.

The next third try hard not to be.

The last third would like to be if only they got the chance.

Trust can only exist where there's a possibility of betrayal. Jealously is inevitable, it goes hand in hand with love. When I tell Le Doux 'I'm not jealous,' the truth is I'M LYING. So how do we fight against the destructive impulse spawned by jealousy? It's not easy, but on reflection, the only way to turn it into something positive is to transform it and turn it to our advantage.

I see, and how do you do that, you may well ask.

In the most horizontal way possible.

The effect of jealousy is to produce an intersection of simultaneously vicious and virtuous circles. Jealousy drives you crazy, so much so that it can inspire you to rekindle your sex life with the same energy you had in the early days. So why deprive yourself of the advantage you gain from feeling you're in competition? Let your body's little cells succumb to agitation, and there's a good chance they'll swing into action on the other side as well. Jealousy is libido's best friend, because desire for something desired by others is an established truth, who knows why. That's the way it is, it's not rational. Desire isn't rational, jealousy even less so. Free will goes into sleep mode, personal judgement is neutralised, your thoughts turn into anarchists, and common sense gets lost in the twists and turns of your imagination.

Being jealous isn't just a slightly crazy, possessive loss of control, or being burdened with a demanding, cumbersome and overblown ego, it's also about feeling more alive than ever, paying attention to everything, to the other person, to other people, to yourself. Being jealous is better than Weight Watchers, you don't want anything sweet or savoury, you forget to have dinner. It makes you slimmer, but you can also lose weight too fast, which is forbidden in our fifties (only too fast mind, losing weight very slowly is fine).

The only way to live with someone is with the trinity

of shared trust: trust in Him, trust in You, and trust in the Relationship. Otherwise, you'll be in hell on a daily basis, which is exhausting.

Of course, if you find a pair of knickers in your bed or a bracelet engraved with someone else's name, you have every right to ask yourself questions. Mistresses who make home visits make sure to leave all sorts of signs designed to cause chaos – make-up bags, pregnancy tests, condoms – and send devastating texts signed off with heart emojis, which are more visible from a distance than ordinary words.

Marital relations enter a new phase from which there's no going back the day that one of you reads the other's texts or emails. Nothing will ever be the same again. The sideways glance, the mouse clicking on the other person's mailbox, signals the beginning of a new tension, which in turn is the precursor to the countdown. Not necessarily the actual end of the relationship, but still the end.

Even if it's tempting, never bite into the apple, never open Pandora's box.

Be warned that once the infidelity comes to light, the mistress is counting on grief, anger and the 'official' partner's ability to set things in motion. And remember in any case that whilst having an unfaithful husband is bad, being a mistress is even worse, guaranteeing torture in the long run.

And here we have a dilemma: is it better to be with someone unfaithful or single without the infidelity? Would you prefer to die of the plague or cholera?

So what should you do? Should you leave him because he's unfaithful?

Leave if you're no longer in love, if you have the courage and the resources?

We only have one life, which is a good reason to live several.

But one after the other.

A textbook case

You're a young fifty-something who's been married since the last century, and on paper, everything's going well.

And yet lately, two or three apparently insignificant details have set some alarm bells ringing. Your husband's ministerial diary has recently been full of various meetings that turn into very important business dinners, and has even had to make a last-minute business trip to China, no less. Your doubts follow the same curve as the statistics and go through the roof when his absences become too numerous. And when he comes back from China exhausted, suffering from irritation that he blames on jet-lag, working too hard and life's injustices, he won't go near you for a while. Or if he does, it will be quick and disappointing. One day, when you happen to glance at his phone screen as if by accident, you intercept a little text message apparently not for your eyes. 'I miss you so much', Bernard seems to be telling someone.

You stay frozen for a while, your brain in reptilian mode, refusing to investigate any further, as you fight the desire to scroll back through the history and face up to the fact that China is a thirty-year-old blonde.

But please, keep calm (which is easy to say), breathe, then call your good friend – the one with the marriage guidance skills. Listen carefully as she tells you: 'My dear, unless you want to get rid of your unfaithful husband, which would be a bad idea, especially in anger ("especially at your age" is the explanation she won't dare come out with straight away), I recommend that you say nothing and do nothing for the moment.' And even if it's more difficult to say that you don't know than not to say that you do know, don't say anything without first thinking and coming up with a strategy.

Watch your husband struggle with his guilt and his trysts, which will turn sour over time, whilst you stay nice and patient, and even if he makes accusations, which every unfaithful man naturally does, try not to change your attitude. Practise your smile by lifting the corners of your mouth, and you'll deal with the hurt (and your future divorce) later. You've got all the time in the world. On the other side, China will be getting impatient, with a long road of wrong turns stretching out before her, scattered with reproaches, which as we know, signal the beginning of the end.

As you wait for things to calm down, take an inconsequential lover. There are plenty of men around who want nothing more, and you'll find them on dating sites, or otherwise in your old address books. Have as much fun as you can, reactivate your old networks, activate some new ones, treat yourself to some body sculpt or ballet fitness classes, visit the latest exhibitions, keep running! Organise dinners out with friends (without specifying that they're female friends) and wait.

Do you reckon he'll come back?

There's also the option of hysteria and rage, which can be effective if your husband was scolded a lot as a child. But you'll need the right temperament, and he'll have to have the right personality. It's a question of compatible neuroses.

The worst thing to do is prevaricate. And the worst of the worst is to spend hours on the telephone to your friends explaining with the help of circumstantial evidence how that bastard was screwing that bitch at a certain point in time. Some of your friends will implore you to leave him and move on, which is a roundabout way of telling you that they don't want to hear about it any-more, that they want you to go back to being you again, as you were before the jellyfish of jealousy had wrapped its sticky tentacles around you and infected you with its bitter sadness. They will spend hours explaining why you should cut yourself off from this toxic individual.

For the sake of your friends, family, children and second cousins, please heed the advice of an experienced young fifty-something: dignity, independence and work on your breathing. If you want to talk, make an appoint-ment. And forget the 'good friend' who won't always give good advice, especially if she's the one sleeping with your husband.

The rivals to watch out for

Now that I'm in a relationship, I don't want anyone taking him away. I had enough trouble getting hold of him. I waited long enough. I pretend to be over it, but the 'tart party' still sticks in my throat, even though we've never spoken about it again.

We have a lovely, sweet life, treat each other with respect and never argue. I've never known such harmony before. I don't know if Le Doux was like that with all his previous partners, but I can assure you that if he was, they must miss him. Because his kind of harmonious living and adaptability aren't that common.

Without fixating on the subject of possessing the object of my love and the fear that someone will steal him from me, I can recognise the fact that these are new anxieties. I used to complain about being on my own, but I'd forgotten how nice it was not to have a rival, not to be in competition. One of the advantages of being single is not to experience the fear of abandonment, the dread of infidelity, of catching a sideways glace. So overnight, you have to come to terms with something new, namely trust.

If you and your beloved live in some far-flung place like Nicaragua, for example, where the standards of beauty are different from our own, good news, you can rest easy, your loved one has little chance of being exposed to someone else's desires, and the same goes for you. But Paris is far more dangerous.

There will always be women who are more beautiful, more elegant, more brilliant, younger, richer or funnier than you, than us, than me. None of them will have all these qualities. But you'll notice these other women at times when the wear and tear of daily life seeps into the gaps in your unshakeable passion.

Men are faithful, not for moral reasons, due to their status, or because of the sincere and eternal love they pledge to their wives or partners, but due to an absence of opportunities. A man can become unfaithful the day he meets someone who deliberately and systematically creates the idea of a possibility. Luckily, the really good-looking ones aren't the most forward, it's usually the ones who don't look that great who go the furthest. And another piece of luck: your partner isn't the object of universal desire.

You'll see some women who play an 'attacking game', with the self-assurance of schemers having fun and with nothing to lose. A burst of laughter is difficult to challenge ('But come on, we're only laughing'). A single attacker will have less chance of attracting interest than a woman who's part of a couple and covers her tracks. In this instance, it might be a sexual game she plays with her partner, who's used to his wife chatting up someone else as he looks on complacently. You never know what goes on in people's heads, or their underwear.

Back home, nicely warmed up by this bit of public play-acting, Monsieur may want to reprimand Madame before passionately expressing his admiration. Everyone has their little tricks, and you can't presume to know how a long-term couple works. Nevertheless, you'll be well within your rights to be annoyed if you see your other half wagging his tail when this slightly tarty little tease feeds him her outrageous come-ons. Because at fifty and beyond, we're more fragile and more easily unsettled

in our relationships. Should we see our partner's recep-
tiveness as a first step towards betrayal? Not necessarily.
But peace of mind is an important thing when we're in
our fifties.

You just need to keep hold of your man, old girl,
thinks the little tease.

But it was just a game, he tells you.

Yes, but I saw you preening, you want to scream.

To bring the situation back in hand sincerely, calmly
and objectively, you should explain how you felt and
demand respect. Then you can forget about it for once
and for all, or only bring it up for a laugh. There's no
point in flying off the handle or getting all reproachful,
it's counter-productive. Hold back your anger, sadness
and fear. You'll find the right words at some point. But if
the little seed of jealousy takes root in your everyday life
thanks to this insignificant event to the point of turning
things sour, you'll need to think things over and assess
the enemy to gauge whether she represents a genuine
threat or not. So first of all, who is she?

If she's a thirty-nine-year-old with no children, you
can rest easy, however bold her seduction plan. Men in
their fifties are suspicious. They've been around the block
and are no longer wet behind the ears. Even if they fall
for her, without a published certificate of sterility not
many would want to go near . . .

Likewise, if the tart trying to chat up your husband is a woman around forty with young children. Other people's kids are only tolerable if they're grown up or not there. The mother of a young child is relegated to the role of mistress or will have to negotiate with the father one week in two to give herself some breathing space.

If she's a forty-five-year-old with pre-teens, she isn't a threat either. Parents' evenings, extra-curricular activities, a time-consuming job and holidays with potential step-children where you're mutually irritated by the differences in their upbringings and personalities can put paid to marital prospects fairly quickly. Oh, so we need a six-room apartment? If their financial footprint, even combined, can't stretch to their requirements for a shared living space, everything very quickly gets complicated.

The potential rival to watch out for, on the other hand, is stunning, independent but spoken for, has no kids and isn't really the right age to have any. The snake in the Garden of Eden would happily put a foot in the door half opened by even a subtle ambiguity.

Few men can resist the insistent attentions of a beautiful woman.

In similar situations, do women have a stronger will? It depends. Everyone needs to be reassured. Everyone likes a little stimulation. There's nothing to stop you climbing up to the ten-metre diving board yourself, enjoying the little thrill of vertigo and . . . going back down by the ladder.

Or you could take a leap and attempt a majestic swan dive. At your own risk and peril. In these cases, it's better not to think, because the pleasure of a roll in the hay or an affair with someone else (man or woman) will always be too short-lived in comparison to the mountain of irreversible problems that arise when infidelity is ascertained, discovered or worse still, admitted! With a little luck and skill, no one will be any the wiser, because whilst the infidelity is the bad news, the good news is that we're only jealous about what we know. Don't worry, it won't change anything, jealousy never makes us leave, it just locks us in a little more.

My personal statistics tell me that we're unequally affected by jealousy, which ruins some people's lives, but luckily, not all men are unfaithful, and not all of them make us jealous. Personally, I'm not of a jealous disposition, but try me and I'll show you a clean pair of heels.

The secret to couples that last

O genie of the lamp, let him be a tiny bit more in love with me than I am with him.

Love is born from the intersection of two obsessions that grow out of the chemistry of the mind and the skin. Then it has a life of its own. It's affected by the phases of the moon, develops over time and wears away before disappearing completely or transforming into something else, another form of love in the best cases, or friendship or affection, according to each person's history or aptitudes.

Going through your life with the wrong person is terrible. How can people come to terms with a mediocre relationship? Only material circumstances and the family unit, which have surreptitiously fossilised over the years by the time we get to our fifties, will prevent us from facing up to it. As for the lack of love, you get used to it by default.

In either case, it's once again a question of fear.

I truly admire couples that last. Those who keep the same partner for life. Defying the wear and tear, keeping their heads up, plugging the leaks from the accumulated years and ensuring that they never take on water. How did they manage to negotiate the crisis of desire and the ways that each partner changed, sometimes in opposite directions? How do they manage to overcome the black hole of the accumulating years? To face up to or resist the various temptations, when they become alluring? Uncharitable souls will highlight the extent to which these inseparable couples are united by a comfortable existence that is difficult to unravel, unless they're bound by compromises that are too firmly embedded or insanity too inextricably intertwined. They have their mystery that makes them work.

Some are lovely to see, benevolent and eternal, dealing well with disagreements, if any arise. Others are terrifying, toxic, fossilised. They struggle to deal with the aftermath of vexation, reproaches or quarrels. The irritation that emerges in a particular tone. How do you wipe away the persistent after-effects of mood swings? They dissolve at different rates depending on different characters, I imagine. On the other hand, people who get along too well are irritating and suspect in equal measure. Is one half of the couple actually a real person?

But I think that if you've managed to overcome the final transitional periods and their challenges – departure of the last child, furtive crushes, discretion, tearful forgiveness – then you'll be together for the long run. For a couple to endure for many years, bound together in happiness, it's preferable for at least one of them to be a very nice person, and for neither of them to be particularly bold.

Marriage

O genie of the lamp, may we always want to but never need to.

At the outset, the point of getting married is to put on an elegant celebration for two people who want to make a song and dance about their sexual compatibility . . .

Let's look at the wedding to begin with: a beautiful and hugely entertaining day, with flowers, gifts and smiles everywhere, and floating in the air, the treacherous thoughts that only emerge at honorific ceremonies.

The light and attention will be focused above all on the Bride, with a capital B, resplendent in her high heels, chignon and Chantilly lace. Her parents will exude the blissful satisfaction of relief, his will be sulking but trying to hide it as best they can. Her single friends will radiate suspect goodwill and turn on their radar: with their music, free bars and well-oiled guests, weddings have always been a much happier hunting ground than any dating site.

People will listen carefully to the speeches made by his juvenile friends, holding their breath in fear of an unfortunate revelation from the past, and after the tedious childhood videos, everyone will applaud heartily. Malicious souls will take bets on how long it will last and the mean-spirited will note the year of the bride's birth when they exchange their vows at the town hall, thinking it was 'about time'.

Whilst marriage is useful in all kinds of ways – only making one tax declaration, having socially legitimate children, accessing various special deals, bringing the marital unit together under a single name, and so on — in the end, its main purpose is to give one partner legal authorisation to press the button on a social elevator that will take them higher than they would have reached on their own. But on the day the vows are exchanged, it is a fairy-tale dream come true.

Then one day, the marriage will really make sense, when one of the two will congratulate themselves for having enshrined their feelings in a legal pact.

Because this is the thing.

Love (often) doesn't last.

Whereas marriage (always) lasts too long.

And let's not even mention divorce, which goes on for ever.

A good reason to get married . . .

If you weren't lucky enough to be born with a surname that's easy on the ears, a truly sexist feature of marriage is to allow you to get rid of the patronym you inherited from your father and replace it with one from your husband. If your childhood bitterness persists (can the woman who holds nothing against her father please raise her hand?), marriage can put an end to this almost daily reminder of paternal influence.

Personally, I've never wanted to make everything official and get married. I'm terrified by the idea of going into a church or a town hall masquerading in white. But if my maiden name happened to be Couillonard* and I chanced to meet a Monsieur de Bourbon Parme, and a sweet romance ensued, I think I would pester the gentleman to marry me. And if the marriage ended in divorce after a few years, my first instruction to my lawyer would be for him to ensure that I was entitled to use my new name for life. Now of course, at key moments such as a child's engagement or the birth of a grandchild, the social pages of *Le Figaro* would always refer to 'Madame de Bourbon Parme née Couillonard', which you'd take as a low blow from your ex-husband.

But leaving aside ugly names or low status, marriage is first and foremost the culmination of boundless love that you wish to express in public through legal means and for statutory purposes.

Footnote: it will also be a way of making it clear to the tart who's busy chatting up your husband that she should take a step back, or even two, and that things will get difficult for her if she carries on prancing and wiggling like that. What we've learnt over the years and

---

* Translator's note: the equivalent of being called something like Miss Ballcock.

from our friends is that the marriage contract contains no fidelity clause. Quite the reverse. There are even specialists, women with a deeply rooted self-hatred, who are mistresses first and foremost and don't aspire to anything else. They're not the most dangerous, but even so.

Prevention is better than cure

Some say that the day divorce is made simpler, people will start getting married again. It's a little like saying that the day firing people is made simpler, people will start hiring again. The family court is to marriage what the industrial tribunal is to paid employment. Except that no one will demonstrate in the streets to relax the laws governing the severance of a marriage contract. At a push, you might see lawyers demonstrating to demand that the process remains as slow, complex and opaque as it currently is.

At the bitter end, possessions and pain will be equitably divided. Because not only does a long-running divorce impoverish both parties, even the one who set the process in motion, it also ruins, paralyses and holds back any reconstruction.

The guilt felt by the one who flies the nest, if the gentleman is the happy unfaithful party, will produce an outpouring of generosity proportional to his partner's rage, but will not necessarily meet with any gratitude. As the court orders are issued, egos will begin to unfurl, and each party will try to give the best account of their role in the story. As things inevitably turn squalid, the enraged party will turn militant, directing his or her thoughts into war. Friends, children and silverware will also be cut in two. Friends and even children will be asked to take sides. The rest will end up at the Saint-Ouen flea market.

Division would be simple if both parties' contributions could be quantified in the same way, but how can you be sure? Divorce opens the door to all kinds of vileness. From the career put on hold to look after the children, to dinner parties held to help advance a partner's career, issues of isolation, time, breast feeding and the provision of stability will have to be taken into account. A judge will have to make a decision that is inevitably unjust. With its judicial timetable and visiting rights, divorce robs you of peace, as each side dwells on their respective grievances and tots up all those things that were freely given when you were in love.

The most positive aspect of divorce is that once it's decreed, if there's nothing left to negotiate, the dust will suddenly settle amidst an indifference that you never would have thought possible. For the greater good, for the sake of balance, children and our finances, and to allow everyone to move on, these procedures must be streamlined. But for the survival of practitioners of family law, it's imperative that nothing changes.

Can you still get married at fifty?

In our fifties, after several lives, marriage isn't even on the agenda. Getting married no longer means much in the Dionysian sense of the term, all the more so as break-ups and past experiences may have dampened our enthusiasm for the benefits of the institution.

No need for specific statistics to tell you that most first marriages end up in a knife fight. And with each side weighed down by tons of baggage, it's best avoided. But if an appropriate and timely part of you still yearns for romance and the absolute, then why not?

I've always thought that before getting married, you need to have done a lot of living. To have known other bodies, experienced a whole range of feelings, to have suffered enough, lost yourself in the tortuous meanders of intoxication, been moved to tears, been able to give your all with no regrets, have laughed in bed, and read afterwards, to have repeated the same mistakes several times, thought about it and understood . . . And if after all that, you still harbour the desire, or even the idea of the desire, it's because you really have found The One.

As well as certainty in love, marriage will always bring a certain status, a sense of protection and the impression of having more weight as a couple, of being stronger, going hand in hand, forming a unit and being able to wear the 'perfect couple' label in the harmonious balance of a dining-room table, to be known as 'The So-and-Sos' ... But it's also a way of strengthening a construction, turning a plan into reality, and after a certain age, things become less unstable. Wherever you go, you go with the foundations of the past.

That said, would we refuse the ring and the framed photo of the big day in the hall?

At an age when our young fifty-something's lives have found their equilibrium, we have no need of someone to have children with, less need of financial support, and we're used to our status. So why say yes?

He'd really have to insist.

Well, actually, he'd have to ask, first of all.

Advice for young women

Love with all your heart whilst asking yourself if your chosen one's qualities will be compatible with the toll that time will take, and the changes in your circumstances and his character, should your love grow weaker. Ask yourself these questions: will I think as highly of him when I love him less (or when he loves me less)? Will he be my companion in good fortune as well as bad? Will he be generous if we break up? Even in the early days of a relationship, you can already have an idea of the answers, even if they're approximate. Watch out for skinflints who spend too long adding up and staring at the restaurant bill, avoid profligates who waste their money showing off or compulsive spenders who collect and accumulate. Consider the hedonist who finds the right balance between needs and pleasure, and keep your distance from those who treat money with contempt when they don't have any.

Above all, girls, study, feed your mind, cultivate your talents, work and don't stop. Always be independent. Beware financial dependency, which locks you in and ties you down.

And never forget that kindness and generosity are two qualities that go through the years intact, whatever the circumstances.

Advice for young men

Set your sights on brave, kind and hard-working girls. Run a mile from princesses and airheads who will leave you in the lurch when the chips are down. Remember that character traits become more pronounced with the passing years. Towers always fall the same way they lean. What's adorable at twenty-five is less so at fifty. With a little luck, you'll be out of the picture by then. If you've fallen out of love with a dependent partner, you drag them behind you for your whole life pretending to be reconciled whilst regretting that your love for them was all too brief. All this in the name of a family model our subconscious supposedly subscribed to.

Buying a gift for a young fifty-something

To paraphrase André Gide, what's important is not what you see but the way you see it. Even so, can someone still remind him that I like peonies in June, mimosa in January and unexpected little surprises all year round.

Gifts lie at the intersection of love, finances and generosity. In your solo years, you didn't have to give or receive gifts, but in a relationship, the issue comes up several times a year: your respective birthdays, Christmas, Valentine's Day, wedding anniversaries or anniversaries of being together . . . A recurring conundrum and boomerang pleasures.

A bag

In Fifty-Something-Land, we generally have everything. But 'everything' includes things that can vary and multiply infinitely. Bags provide a fairly good illustration of the unnecessary materiality of possession. Whether they're handbags, rucksacks or shoulder bags, we never have enough bags and never will. Bags aren't accessories, they're essentials.

Clothes

Whatever you like. Amaze me! As my birthday falls at the beginning of November, I'm afraid anyone buying me designer clothes will have to pay full whack, they're never in the sales. This drawback comes with a supplementary advantage for me: I can always exchange the gift for something else if it doesn't suit me. So I've always had fewer presents than my friend Cosy, who was born around the first day of the sales, on 2 July, but she's never safe from an unwelcome surprise, which she'll have to put up with come what may.

A book

In principle, a book is an inexpensive gift, but will only fit the bill if it's personal and well-chosen. Otherwise, it's often wide of the mark or something you already have. Be nice and don't insult us by giving us books we're supposed to have read. So avoid the classics, with the exception of nice-looking sets of the complete works of whoever you like. A better choice would be the latest prize-winners. Out of politeness, leave the bookseller's label, but exchanges should be prompt. These days, book shops all too frequently turn into organic grocers or hearing-aid shops overnight, and then before long, these newcomers will in turn morph into places in tune with the zeitgeist and the neighbourhood.

Jewellery

Jewellery is hard to exchange without hurting the other side's feelings, but whilst it always creates surprise, it's rarely inappropriate. Unless of course someone buys you earrings when you don't have pierced ears – which is laden with significance. The least you can expect is a simple piece of costume jewellery that's all about the symbolic value. At best, you'll be looking at a suedette box with gold letters, especially if it's done properly and hidden away, so that you discover it in your coat pocket or underneath your napkin in the restaurant. With your hand over your mouth, you'll adopt the look that says, 'what a surprise!' (a disgruntled brain cell will be saying 'about time!'). Before opening the package, you'll turn it round in your hands, then slowly undress it, taking your time, being careful to savour the wait, accompanying these delicate gestures with smiles and little questions so as to prolong the pleasure. Then you'll slide the ring on to the most appropriate finger as you congratulate yourself for having left a note of your most detailed measurements lying around.

An anachronism

Anyone who gives you a CD hasn't heard of Spotify, Deezer or Qobuz, and so must be over forty. It's a bit like a sixty-nine-year-old giving a VHS video cassette to a fifty-year-old friend. You're always one person's geek or another person's dinosaur.

A passport

The most incredible, original gift has to be the one that a Russian oligarch gave to his wife for their tenth anniversary. All done up in a nice presentation box, Madame was delighted to find some genuine new identity documents in her name, but showing her date of birth to be ten years later. And if you say you're born ten years later, you're ten years younger! Money can't buy you everything, but it can still buy a lot. This kind of gift only makes sense if it's accompanied by a battery of injections and the à la carte services of an e-reputation specialist to remove all trace of any compromising information. A high-flying lie requiring schizophrenia and method, as well as the carefully calculated eradication of your close circle of friends. If you want to do something original and you're absolutely determined to give me a new passport with a new date of birth, just for fun, I suggest you get one under a different nationality, from a tiny country, somewhere out of the ordinary like the Vatican City or Andorra, made out in a different name if possible. That way, I'll be able to ask the Community Manager to invent me a new backstory, a new childhood and education, a brand-new past. As for the future, I'll take care of that.

Flowers

The only permitted accounting procedure would be for your partner to give you a bouquet of roses with one flower for each of your birthdays. With a bit of discretion, he could even have the delicacy not to use the exact total. Subtracting a few roses, for example, would be a subtly affectionate gesture. It's not that often that elegance also saves money.

A party

When your birthday comes around, why not go to bed early with your partner, having done justice to the bottle of Ruinart Blanc de Blancs champagne you specially chilled for the occasion, then wake up with a headache, another year on the milometer and one fewer left to live?

But take pity on us, please, no surprise birthday parties. Frankly, we're too old for that sort of thing. The shock of seeing the guests emerge from behind the sofa in high spirits, glasses in hand, isn't good for the heart. And then you can picture the scene: holding back your tears, stifling your embarrassment, dealing with the inevitably disappointing prolonged silence, with that feeling of not being worthy of those who've gone to so much trouble for you . . . At times like this, a speech of thanks is required, ideally delivered with wit, sensitivity and good voice placement. Please let no one close to me get married or die, so that I'll be for ever spared from marriage songs and eulogies: they're not in my programming. At a push, give me a piece of paper and a pencil three days before and I'll write you a poem.

There's also the option of throwing a non-surprise birthday party for your partner, asking them for their guest list, menu, music, present idea and favourite cake. No risks and no surprises. Plans announced in advance have their charm, but the tried and tested approach of an intimate celebration, just the two of you in a classic or unusual setting, will always be my preferred option. A romantic weekend away somewhere will add a stone to the wall of your memories, and if you then find another rock by chance in the pocket of your jacket, comfortably nestling in a little suedette box, that would be a pretty successful birthday, don't you think, Le Doux?

The joys of Christmas?

Christmas is the season of obligatory decorations, unfortunate presents, festive misbehaviour and disruption to your normal mealtimes. It's the season to take stock of your professional and personal life, the end of love affairs that started in early summer, a time for grey, rainy weather, grey, older-looking skin, and for being asked two hundred times between 15 November and 15 December, 'What are you doing for Christmas?' Help! You can only hope that the genie of the lamp comes out from his hiding place, a bottle of champagne in his hand, and says: 'Come on then, my dear, it's open season, give me your wishes.' I'd ask for a pair of size five and a half shoes, another bag, a piece of costume jewellery that still says 'gemstone', a massage in a luxury hotel spa, a course of dance lessons in a European capital, the bestsellers everyone's talking about, and my final request, unless it was the first, would be for my romance to suffer no direct or collateral complications.

With a cheeky sidelong glance, the genie of the lamp would ask: 'Another bag? But you've already got thirty-two!'

'So what's the problem, are you the genie of the lamp or not?' I would reply.

When it's all over, you'll be pleased or disappointed, but in any case relieved to have finally got through this depressing time of year, when hysterical consumerism competes against predominantly greasy and sweet snacks. Then it's time to sort through the presents: the 'already got it', 'don't like it', 'doesn't go', 'not my style' . . . Do you throw them away, regift them or sell them? Internet shopping encourages poorly chosen gifts. But if someone gives me genuine but suspect identity documents, I'll keep them. Who knows if one day the Vatican or the Catalans of Andorra will rule the world . . .

A wrapped present isn't 100 per cent safe. It can be tacky, inappropriate, overgenerous, late or another piece of clutter, but thoughtfulness, imagination, anticipation, surprises, sharing and the special moment when you pull the ribbon slowly towards you before opening the parcel will always feel wonderful.

A poem, a drawing or a song can make more of an impact than a Vuitton bag.

Has this section struck a chord? Do you recognise the way love makes us fragile and pugnacious, sweet-natured and sensitive? The following section goes a little bit further. I want to lift another corner of the rug, before raising the curtain on the things we never mention in public, but always discuss amongst friends. So, my fellow young fifty-somethings, let's stick together and gather round as we take the plunge into our intimate lives. With no censorship.

Everything You Always Wanted to Know About Young Fifty-Somethings

'I decided to be happy because it is good for one's health'

Voltaire

Each day I thank my lucky stars that I'm here tapping out cheeky, funny stories on my computer that sometimes extract a smile. So long as I'm occupied with these trifles, it means everything else is going well.

Everything else is the useful, important stuff that we

forget when life is running smoothly. Our bodies, but also our families, friends, beauty, health, sport . . . These are the subjects at the centre of this fourth 'catch-all' section. And although there's no hierarchy, we'll begin with sex.

Sex

Certain trends you'd never have imagined are regularly identified by social networks, blogs or word of mouth. Because whether it's daily, sporadic or fleeting, sex is there, always there, and never so present as when it's absent.

The quality of the sex and its frequency vary according to parameters that also vary, over which we don't always have control. For men, technique can always improve over the years, but the actual effectiveness of the performance is part of the great debate between nature and nurture. Some say that you don't just happen to be a good lover, you become one. Others are convinced that men are born free but unequal. When it comes to virtuosos, opinions are universal and unanimous, but an average, random guy, the lover next door, the Saturday night man-in-the-street might be described as marvellous by one woman and disastrous by the next. God knows why! Circumstances? Feelings? Pills? Or perhaps sexual compatibility depends upon infinitely subtle parameters of physical and mental chemistry.

In any couple, horizontal compatibility is desirable, but as we've gone past the age for taking a roll in the hay in the afternoon thanks to an available red-blooded male or a rush of hormones, it's not vital either. Average sex is much easier to accept than average love. Footnote: but it helps.

Our advantage as young fifty-somethings is that we have a perfect command of our anatomical geography in every sense. We know the words, the music and the rhythm of the song. It's whispered, intoned or crooned from the first beat of the conductor's baton. The most sensitive areas are naturally brought into play at the beginning, and the familiar giddiness takes hold, without surprises, as we slip happily, cheerfully into a controlled trance.

We can imagine that when we reach these heights, the rush of blood to our nervous system puts a sort of ecstatic smile on our faces that nothing appears to justify. There's no mirror on the ceiling or hidden camera to confirm this (at least I hope not), but I suppose we must really pull some faces at certain points. Sometimes I'm vain enough to be worried about it, but not enough to want to hold back.

Once things are working and Monsieur and Madame are getting along nicely, how often should the deed be done? Will Monsieur's urges fit in with Madame's migraines? And will Madame be feeling frisky when Monsieur isn't tired or suffering a malfunction?

It's good, we like it, it works: these are the three fundamental criteria for couples between the sheets. Because even if our bodies don't have an official sell-by date, time will throw its share of spanners in the works. As women and men in our fifties, we will have to work with what we've got.

Those in an official couple balance their sex lives according to the tyrannical triangulation of libido, sleep and laziness. You keep your libido healthy through love, fantasies and certain food supplements prescribed by the right people. The issue of sleep can be solved by going to bed earlier, and taking a little nap in the afternoon. Laziness is the most dangerous. Along with its cousin habit, it's the one you need to fight.

Single young fifty-somethings don't want to spread themselves too thin. Above all, they're looking for a shoulder to lean on, although if it comes with a working appendage attached, they'll undoubtedly be delighted to express the full extent of their gratitude. Single fifty-somethings of the male of the species will be looking above all for moments of pleasure, if possible with no strings attached. And they're more inclined towards young women, who may not be satisfied with either the shoulder or the appendage. (Something you might like to remind them of.)

Assume the position

O genie of the lamp, censored.

You need to revise the classics. The missionary is effective, but the cowgirl is no longer permitted. We're no longer of an age to be viewed from below, except in complete darkness. Similarly, I don't recommend positions exposing our knees to prolonged friction or bumping against surfaces like parquet floors, seagrass or polished concrete. Carpet is no better: you might think the soft wool would be comfortable, but neither luxury materials nor our joints are what they once were. Skin irritation and back pain are guaranteed. If you want to spice things up, look elsewhere.

Come up with some accessories, but have them to hand before the festivities begin (once the engine's running, no one's arm is long enough or available enough to grab them). And don't leave your belongings lying around, it could be a shock for the family unit. Children, of whatever age, cannot conceive of their parents having a sex life. Discovering or observing its existence is a form of torture, let alone discovering the flavour enhancers. So hide everything. Setting aside the trauma, you could find your authority undermined.

Restoke your sleepy imagination, explore the alternatives, revisit the fundamentals. Think about words, which are incredibly effective: my own vocabulary has taught me that some of them count triple. Dig out a peacock feather, a violin bow or a make-up brush and tell him to amaze you or make you squirm, just for a laugh, or maybe not.

Indulge in intra-marital relations. What's that you say? I'm talking about a form of permitted mental adultery, in which you invite anyone you want into your thoughts. There's a playful aspect to it but also a dimension of sharing. All sorts of people you know can visit you in your most intimate moments through images or words. The local cheesemonger, the Turkish guy from the dry cleaners, the woman from the second floor, Brad Pitt . . .

Whisper invitations: Monsieur and Madame are receiving. After you've lived together for a certain time, and desire has started to play by its own rules, putting your taboos on mute isn't so absurd. Does it bother anyone?

On the home straight, on your back in the frog pose or in the cobra pose on your forearms, your intra-marital relations are the little push that shows you seventh heaven from above, the little spark that blows away your remaining dignity, the fire that floods through your body at that precise intimate moment when your voice grows hoarse. Your sex life discreetly accommodates this surprise virtual guest, male or female, and there is nothing to stop you inviting them in, particularly if the object of your fantasies provides effective satisfaction. After all, who will complain? Surely not your partner. If you keep the trick to yourself, there's no need to go into personal details and give jealousy the opportunity to get involved.

Any woman who claims that she hits the jackpot every time, that every shot hits the bullseye, is either a liar or obnoxious. Orgasm is a bonus, and it's normal not to get there sometimes. What's sad is never getting off. Clearly, you can't keep the thermostat turned up to ten all the time without the risk of blowing up the boiler, but if you have your hand on the remote and you're controlling the temperature, easy does it girls!

Love in a hot climate

If you have no sexual partner or you live in Sweden or northern Brittany, you can ignore this section. In either case, you don't have to deal with sweltering summer sex. But for the rest of you, this is my advice for avoiding the drawbacks of intense heat. Depending on the number of years you've been together, you have several options, all of them sizzling hot.

Use tried and tested positions that keep skin contact

to a minimum and erogenous contact to a maximum, postures that turn their back on seemliness and offer both partners mental orientations that can fill in some unexplored areas in the imagination. Hitch up your legs, relax your back, grab some ice cubes to play with and try a game of sexual tit for tat. A sort of tacit agreement guaranteeing a mutual return on investment.

Have a large glass of iced Perrier to hand, and keep a little mouthful longer than expected for a 'frizzante' effect. For those who love their food, the mango and passionfruit sorbet variation is a colder and sweeter option that always hits the spot. Just remember to clear away the remains of the desert so as not to get it all over the bed.

But when your personal heat levels rise and neither of you will consider forgoing the classic release, whatever the temperature outside, fair enough, just go for it. If you do, take a cold shower just before, so that the inevitable suction effect of your chests rubbing together as your two saturated bodies become one is delayed as long as possible. When the slipperiness gets too much, make an effort to speed things up. Cut your usual timescale in half. A little thing like thirty-six degrees won't stop you.

You might also decide it's too hot to think about mixing bodily fluids. If so, wait for the temperature to drop before resuming any sexual activity worthy of the name. Whatever happens, watch out for mirrors lying around. They say it's not good feng shui to have one facing the door in your bedroom, but above all, it can reveal viewpoints that you can't control and would rather hide at your age. Beware the sideways views that you might not notice but can be right there in your partner's line of sight. Whether or not there's a mirror, in textbook positions, the spare tyre is never visible. But anything more flamboyant is liable to present your partner with an image not approved by your censors.

Don't forget the light, which can never be soft enough, or turned off enough. My advice is to keep a little reading lamp lit on the bedside table, or a perfumed candle, which will give out a pretty light but will need vigilance. You want things to be smoking hot, but only figuratively.

P.S. Note to my children: I outsourced this part of my book to a funny, crazy friend of mine, because as you can imagine, I'm entirely incapable of writing this sort of thing, and in any case, I've no idea what she's talking about.

Friends with benefits and easy lovers

Friends with benefits are friends who are sometimes lovers. Compared to sex in a loving relationship, it's like a Blanquette de Limoux compared to Ruinart Blanc de

Blancs champagne, a likeable poor relation. This fun, consensual form of relationship develops with the easygoing relaxation that nurtures the bonds of friendship, which can be strengthened in exchange for a good time. No strings, no one gets hurt. Friends with benefits are often playing on familiar ground, having been in a relationship when they were young. And then life took its course and they lost touch before one day being reunited.

Various sociological ingredients encourage these easygoing relationships: difficulties with commitment for some, the glacial paralysis caused by a brutal divorce for others. These relationships are not binding, they offer nothing new, no surprises, and there's no hunting involved. So how does a friend with benefits differ from an official mistress? The former only has good intentions: the only risk in making love with a friend is playful indulgence, or at most a little spice in the lukewarm water. Whereas the lover/mistress relationship has its own rules and its own law, with a latent potential that can lead from easy-going fun to sadness and war. The relationship, stamped with a seal reading 'between consenting adults', begins with a moment of madness, before you find yourself receiving texts along the lines of 'Shame, I'd made boeuf bourguignon', and can then descend into an irreversible act of war, like a phone call to the wife or an anonymous letter.

How does your bedpost look?

We all have our share of embarrassing past transgressions. You know what I'm talking about: the whirlwind fling ('just the once') with the bloke you REALLY didn't want anyone to know about ('was it him that told you?'), when one fine day ('well, it was a long time ago'), due to a misunderstanding ('there wasn't a single taxi') and/or strenuous efforts ('he spent hours chatting me up, I can't tell you how hard he tried') you let your hair down ('it was just a case of right time, right place'). We're prepared to use any justification ('we didn't really go the whole way'), any excuse ('I'd had a bit too much of the Saint-Julien') or shoddy explanation ('I was only paying that other shit back for screwing around'). Some will even go as far as to deny it ('I swear nothing happened') or turn it into something trivial ('if that's what happened, I don't remember'). Just remember that history always catches up with us. Why? Because the world is such a small place.

When I say 'we all', I'm talking about women, because the same doesn't apply to men. I've noticed that no man is ever ashamed of getting his leg over, even with the ugliest woman in the neighbourhood. A healthy number of conquests, no matter who they are, will always improve a gentleman's status, whereas a lady will lose her mystery, unless there are some recognisable names amongst her liaisons.

It's terrible, I know, but some conquests lift you up (Brad P, George C, Benjamin B . . .), whereas some drag you down (luckily, not everything's in the public domain). Our image depends in part on the quality of the notches on our bedpost, past and present. So when the rumour circulates that you've been involved with a 'celebrity', whether it's a Hollywood star or a provincial politician, the invitations arrive, your popularity increases, and hesitant suitors suddenly come out of the woodwork.

I know one woman in her fifties who's free, fun to be with, resolutely single, and quite happy to reveal the names of her conquests to anyone and everyone. At first, I didn't really understand it. But when one of my friends, a big name in politics, said he went back to hers one night even though he hadn't been interested before, I realised that she was an expert in her field and was using them as bait.

A few months ago, thinking we could go out and have some fun, or under the (mistaken) impression I had an address book full of celebrities, she suggested a drink at the Café de Flore – I say a drink, she immediately ordered a bottle! With each name she mentioned, my eyes grew a little rounder: 'Oh really, him as well! So how long did that go on?' The out of the blue, she asked me: 'What about you, who's the most famous person you've slept with?' (True story, I swear.)

ME Err . . .

HER What do you mean, 'err'?

The absence of any horizontal celebrity action in my life seemed so incongruous, so pathetic to her that I detected something akin to pity through the alcohol in her eyes. Next thing I knew, she downed the rest of her drink, telling me she'd forgotten two things: an imminent meeting and her purse.

'See you soon,' we said as she left.

I never saw her again.

The ex who reappears

It's always at the point when you're head over heels in love with your absolute Dream Guy, and you intend to maintain a certain veil of obscurity over your past, that an ex suddenly springs up out of nowhere. We can trust the likes of Google, Facebook, Twitter or LinkedIn to bring them to the surface and allow them to gravitate in concentric circles that we'd sometimes like to be able to direct elsewhere.

There he is, in a group of mutual friends, all smiles. He spots you and pounces. Introductions are made, his conspiratorial wink is already getting on your nerves, and you have your fingers crossed that he'll avoid any reference to the past in front of Dream Guy. But as we said, he's the Dream Guy, he's cool with it.

On the face of it, an ex is someone we'd like to see disappear from the face of the planet. It only takes a few sentences for you to remember why you left him. Personally, I've got two or three I'm more than a little proud of, but just as many (more, even) I'd be prepared to swear with my head on the block that I've never met. At a certain point in my life, I had dependably poor taste. But come on, admit it, we all have something similar in our unofficial biography, don't we?

Nevertheless, there are good and bad exes.

A good ex is someone you broke up with, who was cut up about it but remained dignified and was always a little nostalgic about those days, when the arrogance of beauty and youth gave you the power to sweetly mistreat him.

The bad ex is the same thing, but with the boot exactly on the other foot. Perhaps I'm not being very clear, but I'm sure everyone understands.

In the case of the good ex, the break-up was a calm affair: two or three early warning signs, no more, followed by a dinner somewhere nice, a gift on the plate, a few compliments with the aperitif and suddenly, with the fork on the way to the mouth, quick as a flash, a clean cut with no rough edges. The one wielding the secateurs contritely says: 'You deserve to be loved so much more', leaving the other one furious at not having been the first to pull out this poignant line. Once the last mists of pride have evaporated, friendship could even develop.

Ten years later, the good ex is still there. We've given up trying to get rid of him, he's part of the furniture. He even greets the Dream Guy with a kiss on the cheek, which is the way the boys do it on the Rive Gauche . . . He's at all the parties and will even serve the wine. The Dream Guy isn't jealous, which is his smallest defect.

Family life

Fifty is the age of repeated family upheavals. Some things are resolved, but others unravel. The children have left, and the parents are at sea. But let's keep our heads up and try not to fall into the trap of nostalgia.

Where have our children gone?

O genie of the lamp, I want to be teleported back twenty-five years to the school play (and actually get there on time).

For years, they filled the house with their presence and their soundtrack of tears, laughter, shouting and general noise, not to mention the draughts . . . Did we tell them we loved them enough when they were young? Because we were always snapping at them for insignificant things: 'turn that TV down/you've been played those games too long/that's enough cake/stop squabbling . . .'

What a guilty relief it was on Monday morning when the nanny arrived, or we dropped them off at school! Taking care of two young children after a hectic week of work and stress was so tiring, I remember wishing the weekends were shorter and the naps longer. You had to go to the park, keep tabs on them, put them in fancy dress, come up with activities, put up with puppet shows . . . I'd have preferred to meet up with my single friends for a shopping safari, take a dance lesson or simply do nothing. So we negotiated with the fathers, and kept checking our watches. Nap time's over already, here they are again.

And then one day, they're adults and they're leaving home. They've gone.

We even helped them on their way, but as is often the case, we said the opposite of what we were thinking, pretending to be delighted they were leaving. Suddenly, the house was empty of their noise and we started to miss what used to be so annoying. They took their music and their mess with them, and the laughter went too.

Since then we've spent our lives running after them, and negotiating opportunities to see them. We suggest all sorts of things, from various celebrations to trips to increasingly far-flung destinations. Any excuse to share some moments together. So they grant us a little of their time, but now they're the ones looking at their watches. They're in a hurry, with their own lives that they're making without us. We don't even have a say. At best, they'll keep us informed.

What to do with all this love that's become a burden to our children?

Some parents get a dog or a cat, take a lover or medication. Most of all, we'll need time to get used to their absence and their sporadic visits.

After a while, a new rhythm and rituals emerge. Our children don't realise how much these moments mean, but we savour them more keenly, like a gift from above. Long gone are the days when the parents would be congratulated when the children came down to say hello to their dinner guests dressed in flannelette pyjamas, before disappearing back to their rooms. There was also a reluctance to talk about difficult children, but when one mother started to spill the beans about her offspring's misbehaviour, everyone chipped in with their stories, relieved at not being the only ones to feel useless and powerless in their role as average mothers. What I find most reassuring is to tell myself I did what I could. But the truth is I could've done better.

Couldn't we just go back a tiny bit?

What wouldn't I give for a puppet show in the park. I've got time now.

Oh, it's not possible, you say?

Our children are now a distant, abstract presence. They're there, and not there. When people ask us what they're up to, we give a quick résumé of their achievements with undisguised pride. Modestly acknowledging the reaction: 'Oh fantastic, well done.'

We swallow our reproaches and avoid telling them we'd like them to call more often, for no reason, just to ask how things are going, just to say hello, and nothing else.

No, we bite our tongues.

How long has it been since we called our own parents?

How to cope with ageing parents

At some time in our glorious fifties, a period of major upheavals for some of us, most of which have yet to be resolved – separation, divorce, career slowdown, children leaving home, lovers coming and going, etc. – we find ourselves having to deal with the issue of our parents.

Before thirty, children are the parents' problem, and

after fifty, parents are the children's problem. Sometimes, they live independently for years, luckily for them and for us. But what do you do when everything goes downhill? Sign them up for a four-star serviced apartment or the nearest nursing home, take on three 24-hour home helps cash in hand, or put in a request for help from the local social services? Unless you can make a bit of room for Granny and Grandpa and set aside the downstairs bedroom. As their children we have a duty to support them. But it becomes a family problem, because if having your semi-incapacitated parents come to live with you could turn into a bad dream (with rare exceptions), having your in-laws move in spells nightmare (without exception).

With a little luck, you mother-in-law was sprightly enough to look after your children when they were young, but with even better luck, both in-laws were kind enough to pop their clogs after that. If anyone thinks I'm being horrible, please fill me in on your personal situation. Ah yes, I thought as much, you're not affected.

Lucky you if you have lots of brothers and sisters and healthy finances. If so, there are many solutions. You'll need a family meeting to discuss the options and make a decision.

But otherwise, what do people do? What do normal people do?

In any event, if you're fifty or over, mathematically

speaking, your parents won't be in great shape. It's either the head or the legs, sometimes both. So we summon up all of our goodwill and suffer their misfortunes in silence.

And this is where I get stuck. Because making light and joking about the preoccupations of newly fledged fifty-somethings is OK when it comes to things like love, age, wrinkles and cellulite. But finding the humour in the plight of your ageing parents is hard.

Health issues are daily and never-ending, and when the end does come, it's sometimes long and drawn-out. You have to banish all bad thoughts, and find yourself in the strange position of having to watch their physical and mental decline, powerless to do anything.

One day, the way I saw my parents changed dramatically. I stopped being afraid of them, stopped feeling sorry for them and refusing to judge them, which was what they'd taught me or forced me to do. Instead, I saw them as they were: elderly, weakened and defenceless, shackled to their past, which they returned to almost on a loop, whoever they talked to. These constant reminiscences have gradually submerged a present-day existence that only has room for what's going on in their immediate surroundings: 'the vegetable soup's ready', 'the cat's on the terrace', 'we haven't seen the tortoise for three days', 'my cousin stopped by this morning', 'she's the only one still alive', 'all my friends are dead'. The obituaries section is the first bit of the newspaper they read, to catch up with the news, and funerals have become the new focus for the final act of their social life. So we go to see them, for their sake and the sake of our conscience. We listen to them or pretend to listen to them, giving them back the time they gave us. But time weighs heavy, treads water, as if it could dissolve into memories. They try to move us, to stimulate our compassion, when we are more inclined to simulate it, sorry to discover we don't have that much.

And we feel so helpless when faced with the wreckage of their lives. And so distant. They never talk about us, about what we were, what we've become, they only talk about themselves. We're just a reflection of them that they've lost control over. We're amazed at their cynical view of death, about which they feel only banally indifferent.

How do we forgive their failings, how do we bring up everything we've tried to deal with over the years on all the psychiatrists' couches in the world? How do we make our memories less spiky, our recollections fonder? How do we leave only respect and gratitude?

At fifty, we're supposed to be at peace with our parents. No more shifting blame for our failures, it's no longer our parents' fault if . . .

Now, in our fifties, EVERYTHING is our fault. Our

tumultuous love lives aren't the result of our shaky upbringings. In their hour of weakness, there can be no question of presenting them with the bill for our neuroses, with their excessive inheritance tax.

When it's my turn, mix me up a little cocktail of drugs so I can choose when to go (tell me where to sign), only to be used if necessary, or better still bring me enough hard drugs to end my life in sweet oblivion. But a retirement home: NO WAY! Seeing my poor mother sitting there in her wheelchair breaks my heart, even though she seems quite happy doing her colouring and making her rag-dolls with her friends, who are all in the same state.

I hope that whether I'm chasing my tail or chasing the dragon, with a protracted smile on my face, and a halo of renewed faith, I will still have the desire and the energy to write happy missives on my new blog about the joys of being eighty.

Making peace with your parents, saying I love you

Last year, I went to see my father in the village where he's lived for eighty-nine years. Since my mother's been in a retirement home, he's struggled to cope with the resulting loneliness. In his sometimes disjointed words, I can sense an anger that comes and goes. As someone for whom joy and optimism are a non-negotiable way of life, these visits are a challenge. I've always been in conflict with him. I could never stay longer than four days and rather than face family meals, I preferred to avoid them.

That day, as he came out with his usual fairly biting criticism, rather than move away, I came closer and said very softly in his ear, 'Dad, I love you.'

Why did I say it? What came over me?

I felt it was the only way to sop his barrage of accusations.

And you know what? It worked.

He stopped. A moment passed in silence.

Then he looked at me, as if in a daze, took me in his arms and said with a sob, 'But why didn't you tell me that before MOTHER? Why?'

I could have put him straight, reminded him I was his daughter, not his mother, but his words revealed something so enormous that I couldn't say anything at all. It was like suddenly reinterpreting a whole life, a childhood starved of love, his, mine, the impossibility of passing on what we haven't known. I was left stunned.

At that very same moment, I thought about my children, and was filled with a surge of intense love for them.

Your spiritual side

The current fashion is for the present moment: you have to be firmly anchored in the *here* and fully experience the *now*. According to every psychology magazine, newly qualified life coach or good friend learning mindfulness, living in the present moment is the pinnacle of any kind of personal development. We train ourselves to become a compact mass, breathing and cohabiting with a mind that accepts its emotions, its suffering and its being in their entirety.

Yet it's always in these intimate or meditative moments that the little thing we'd happily do without makes an appearance and jams up the system. I try to sort through my emotions selectively and file recent events that loom large in their proper place in the hierarchy. I try to raise my thoughts as high as possible without them hitting the ceiling. In vain.

The meditation experience

We were in a restaurant, nicely decked out and run by two Peruvian girls who'd studied in Norway. On the menu: salmon ceviche and a meditation lesson. This was the venue chosen by a women's magazine for a gathering of influencers to promote the release of an audiobook with the strange and intrusive title *Inhabiting My Body*.

I admit I have a tricky relationship with meditation, like all serious things where it's not clear what's at stake, but I agreed to behave myself for the friend who'd treated me to the experience.

Sitting up nice and straight, with my hands on my thighs, I listened attentively, barely able to repress my raised eyebrow, and remained in this vaguely curious position, listening, holding my breath, on the verge of a laughing fit.

One thing that is certain and recognised by its devotees is that meditation is incompatible with any form of humour. No one was there for a laugh. We were there to be aware of our sensations, to feel our presence and the presence of the other people in the room. 'Can you feel them?' asked the meditation teacher. I bit my tongue, hoping to keep it together. How did the others manage not to burst out laughing?

During the session, the teacher kept his eyes open and directed his gaze at a specific point, encouraging us to do the same. He was wearing yellow shoes that matched his jacket, and I wondered who sold yellow pumps for men, and more importantly, who bought them? The answer to the second part was in front of my eyes, on his feet.

That was it, my mind was wandering, I was losing it. Returning to concentration wouldn't be that easy, especially if I carried on staring at that yellow point in space. The teacher had a name that sounds like a medicine, a detail I found reassuring. He'd written several bestsellers and founded a reasonably successful meditation school, where you can follow a six-day course entitled 'How to practise loving kindness'. He exuded a natural authority that discouraged any argument. So when a poor woman asked him what the point of meditation was, she got a *mandala* right between the eyes.

'Do you realise how much violence there is in your question?' he replied.

Long pause

'Why do think it should have a point? Why does everything have to have a purpose? Can't we break away from the utilitarian side of things? Don't try to use meditation for your own ends, just be happy to meditate.'

End of questions. Back to meditation.

I was told to welcome in the words, to accept my emotions, to explore my mindfulness, to say hello to my body. I did everything I was told, being carried along by his guiding voice. I became a strand of seaweed, floating on the current, letting go of the reins and letting my mind take flight. My emotions dissolved and, very mindfully, I couldn't help doing a few sums. I thought about his bestselling books, the audiobooks, the school, the seminars, corporate training contracts, perhaps tie-in products, why not some merchandising, documentaries, licences, T-shirts . . . I'd begun with mental concentration and ended up with a business plan in my head. I didn't want to use anything for my own ends, but all the same, it seemed there was a canny businessman surfing the wave.

Le Doux was preparing to endure a day's fasting the next day and didn't know we were going to listen to the first part of the special meditation audiobook that very evening.

I was going to suggest we inhabited our bodies with loving kindness.

I imagined he'd agree.

The programme lasts five hours. We'd probably have plenty of time to come up with some sort of business plan afterwards.

Chloé, fifty-four, serial devotee on a higher plane

Chloé is someone who'll sign up to any available spiritual organisation or community. I'm impressed by her ubiquitous mysticism. How has she managed not to be lured into a sect? In fact, she's had several near misses. She's an old friend I adore, whom I'll stick by for ever, but I take a slightly suspicious view of the alternative distractions she suggests. The other day, for example, she told me she was going to a party on Saturday evening. 'Whose party?' is the logical question that always follows this kind of announcement amongst close friends. 'It's a meditation party,' she told me.

'Great! So what does that involve?'

'We're going into the forest to thank the trees. We'll speak to the universe. The idea is to look for synchronicity, and the next day, we'll see what the universe's answer was.'

OK.

This particular fifty-something has always taken an à la carte approach to her spiritual needs. She has always been an assiduous follower of all sorts of mystical and religious movements. Over the years, she has been convinced of the need to embrace a succession of religious rituals (as well as plenty of trees), but only for a certain time, which often coincided with a love story. As each chapter in her life closed, she appeared to cancel her subscription and take out another.

So for a long time, her religion was Judaism. She studied the Torah, observed the sabbath, avoided prawns and fasted for Yom Kippur. Of course, her initial inspiration was a direct consequence of sharing a bed with a handsome young Jewish boy. He was deeply in love with her, but hadn't dared tell her that his parents would never agree to him marrying a 'goy'. After years of living together and Rabbinical studies, just before her conversion and marriage, he disappeared, leaving my friend temporarily inconsolable. Amongst the various caterers' quotes she'd started to examine, she found a letter from her ex-mother-in-law-to-be, telling her son it was time to explain to the poor girl that she was wasting her time. The letter even went on to suggest a number of suitable marital prospects.

The next significant other was a fervent but moderately practising Catholic, and even though she hadn't really been baptised, the problem was solved with a few catechism classes. Out went Rosh Hashanah, Sukkot, Hanukkah and the rest, and in came Monday evening vigils with the Gospel of St John and spiritual retreats arranged by her diocese. She even suggested I went with her on the Cotignac mothers' pilgrimage. Three days of walking, spurred on by a daily mass, the sacrament of reconciliation and meditations on the rosary. All topped off with a nocturnal adoration. Given my sense of otherness, my religious upbringing and a measure of curiosity, I might have accepted, but three days . . .

These days, Chloé is a Buddhist, which I found out not long ago when I discovered a sort of doll's house sitting in the middle of her living room.

'It's my altar,' she explained.

Oh yes, of course, the altar.

'It's to venerate my "enlightened" self. I've just signed up for a spiritual retreat at a Buddhist centre. Fancy coming?'

Chloé regularly walks round her apartment endlessly chanting her mantra '*Nam Myoho Renge Kyo*', as her teenaged daughters look on, accustomed to it by now, but still amused.

'It's the Lotus Sutra,' she explains. 'The power of prayer over the mind. It's like taking drugs. You don't need antidepressants or wine.'

I think I'll stick with the wine.

In search of meaning

When the things that took up the most of our time – children, relationship, work, etc. – are no longer part of our lives, nature, fearing a vacuum, finds immediate substitutes. We recreate rituals and reinvent habits: gardening, adoption, writing a novel, social media, contemporary art, further education, a new passion, and also religion, which can accommodate all the rest.

Chloé's choices, for example, are to do with a desire to belong to communities in which she finds the family structure that she missed so much. But other people's reasons may be different. It's not uncommon for religion to start to play a bigger role at fifty. We go back to the church, synagogue or temple, places that we slightly neglected as our family grew. I can see plenty of examples of this return to good faith around me.

In my early years, Sunday mass was like a cheaper form of babysitting. My mother happily sent me off, her mind at ease, and in the meantime, redid her hair, prepared lunch, darned socks . . . As for me, in the large church in the little village where I grew up, kneeling at the prie-dieu with my grandmother's name inscribed on a ceramic plaque, I spent an hour and a quarter adding to my tally of little sins. I daydreamed whilst gazing at the madonnas, sung in Latin at the top of my voice without any idea what the words meant, and to cap it all, pretended to put the coins my mother gave me into the collection. Instead, I spent the money on a ton of sweets, then owned up to my dreams, theft and greed at confession. This not very Catholic behaviour left me with plenty of fillings and perhaps a certain creativity due to all that time with my head in the clouds. For me, mass was a sort of decompression chamber, almost a window of freedom.

Then came the black hole of indifference to any form of religion. But now, I've made my little pact with spirituality in general and the Catholic religion in particular. Without going into detail about my beliefs, I feel in step and in my proper place at moments when I'm almost suffused with peace, equilibrium and serenity.

Here in Paris, the tedious, droning homilies of my childhood are a distant memory, and I'm revisiting these experiences in a different light. The two priests who spoke last Sunday, when I went to mass with one of my friends, were quite dishy young forty-somethings, and frankly brilliant orators. They served up a spirited, inspired sermon, without notes or earpieces, that would have made any public speaking coach proud. They say the churches are deserted and faith is in decline. Maybe, but there are places where on Sunday mornings, in the peace of Christ, people are jostling for space.

I always leave mass with my soul cleansed, my emotions calmed, my conscience lighter and a repentant fervour . . . all the better to get right back to the urban vanities that are so happily familiar without a shred of guilt.

A little while ago, just before I met Le Doux, oppressed by a sense of threatening emptiness, a little hurt once again by a man who didn't want to take things further and influenced by a friend who seemed so happy with her incense sticks and nocturnal mantras, I was gripped by a desire to bring a bit more spirituality into my life.

With no real idea whom to pray to, I got it into my head to explore different religions and their places of worship. The choice was quickly made, and I won't shock anyone when I tell you that some religions are more welcoming than others.

Initially, I wanted to go on a spiritual retreat, and Amma's ashram seemed the sexiest option. I liked the idea of dressing in white, finding God and being hugged by an Indian woman with something of the guru about her. In the end, I went to Kerala on my own and stayed in a hotel on the beach where I could nurse my depression at my own convenience.

The little pleasures of simple things

Why are we always drawn to complicated unhappiness when simple pleasures are close at hand? Each day, we should observe the details of our surroundings, not missing anything. An exercise that allows us to take stock, come into the light and to take a snapshot of events that are more diverting than they might seem. So when I have a little knot in my stomach that won't go away, I try to take pleasure in the simple, almost invisible things around me.

Marvelling at a sunrise, noticing a particular fragrance,

searching your memory (where did I come across that before?), concentrating on the taste of our food and the flavour of love, enjoying yourself when the shop-keeper asks if you'd 'like anything else with that?', being intrigued by the strange gloves that the Japanese tourist is wearing as shoes, allowing your gaze to wander off down a street, deciding to take a mental photograph of a landscape you'll never forget, succumbing to the intoxi-cating slowness of this infinitely discreet observation, looking up to see the beauty. Trying to take a note of one remarkable thing every day. Or two.

And then being satisfied with what life offers us, and above all, being moved by the kindness of others. A timely observation, because as I'm writing these lines, the teenager who lives with us half of the time has just brought me a cup of Japanese tea and some chocolate biscuits. She didn't have to, and I'm blown away by her kindness. But then again, she's not Le Doux's daughter for nothing.

In a similar vein, my friend Chloé, who changes religion like she changes husbands, told me how much fulfilment she got from distributing smiles in the street.

'What do you mean distributing smiles in the street? To who?'

'Well, I smile at the people I pass in the street. You should try it, it does you the power of good. It's a way of expressing your gratitude to the world.'

Chloé's a very good-looking woman and I'm amused to imagine the misunderstandings she might cause amongst the men she passes in the street and smiles at, unambiguously and for no reason.

In this day and age, when harassment in the street and the grey area of consent are hot topics, is it really a good idea? I don't think I'm ready yet to experience everything that other people find fulfilling . . .

Fashion

O genie of the lamp, let me always be the same dress size, just so I can keep my Hedi Slimane-era Dior suit, which I bought full price on the first day of the sales.

How to sort through your wardrobe

Our idea of style is based on three influences: the press, the street and our friends. Added to this are two factors: our budget, which makes the whole thing possible, and the way we see ourselves.

In our fifties, we have a different relationship to our bodies, to fashion and to clothes than we had in our twenties or thirties. These days, we can legitimately wonder about the age limits for stepping out in leggings, a miniskirt, thigh-high boots, a bra without underwire, a backless top (with no bra at all) . . .

Who will tell us it's too late? A good friend?

'Sorry hon. High boots and a miniskirt is a difficult look when you're the wrong side of forty and the wrong side of size twelve.'

Who can really give objective, neutral, friendly advice?

At a certain point, or gradually, we all end up mourning for what we used to wear in our youth. But it's so difficult to resist the knack those Swedish and Spanish clothing firms have of filling up our wardrobes with things we almost never wear!

These days, recent purchases are about 'safe, everyday' items that we mix with our personal collection of antiques. They've accumulated over the years like layers of sediment packed into our wardrobes and we haven't known how to or haven't been able to get rid of them. All these useless, unfashionable old clothes that we don't know what to do with are only there thanks to a label or the persistence of a memory. How can we get rid of the sentimental presence of the Alaïa suit we were given in 2002? Or the pair of size eight trousers we've had for thirty years and hope to be able to put on one day whilst still breathing normally?

We need to be able to off-load the outfits that are no

longer appropriate for our increasing age, the changing fashions, a silhouette that expands the minute we drop our guard and our changing professional circumstances.

But how?

It's a really tricky one.

We need to get burgled.

This would solve our failure to make a decision about all these clothes that we have no opinion on. That are never worn, but refuse to leave and stay there, glued to their hangers.

Selling is the best option. Killing two birds with one stone, you empty out your wardrobe and make some money. There's no law against putting a little extra in the kitty. Specialist sites will take your clothes. Well, not all of them: prepare to be annoyed when your beloved Kenzo outfit is refused with a polite note reading something like: 'We cannot accept this garment, which is not in tune with our customers' requirements', in other words 'we're not interested in your unfashionable old tat'. The problem with selling things online is time. You have to take photos, describe the item, compare it with similar products, set a price and wait. Throwing things away is also a good option for the lazy. Put all your excess clothes in a 100-litre bin bag and out it goes on to the pavement. But beware, this is often an impulsive decision that can lead to eternal regrets.

And this is exactly why we keep everything, to protect ourselves from regrets. We first need to jettison the idea of regret to help us dump our old clothes. It's the same with love. Give! Take the trouble to give. You'll give someone pleasure, and it's always nice to be thanked. Or put them in the cellar/loft in the hope that one day you'll exhume these tons of clothes, maybe when you next move, or you're finally ready to sell them, chuck them or give them away.

I realise that as time goes by, I'm less and less obsessed with buying things, less impatient for the sales, less inclined to go shopping. In fact I'm more likely to say to myself, 'Fancy that, the sales are here already', like a seasonal marker of passing time. Yet despite my superhuman efforts to get rid of my clothes, I carry on replacing things, then look at my dressing room bursting at the seams and the chests of drawers I struggle to shut with dismay.

What's the point of sucking the planet dry to produce more wool and more cotton if we always wear the same clothes? The fashion these days is mainly about not accumulating stuff. I have two or three outfits that are quite simply me, that I feel good wearing. Because at my age, I don't know if I've found myself, but I know what suits me, and I know how I like to present myself: a pair of jeans, a striped top, a jacket, with different materials and sleeve lengths depending on the temperature, and heels or not depending on how far I have to walk.

A young fifty-something in technicolour

Cosy is one of the most radiant fifty-somethings I know. Good-looking, funny and sunny, her humour and wit can transform any leaden party atmosphere. I've always thought that her consistent good humour was a symptom of the good manners, politeness and delicacy with which she treats the world. She refrains from venting or complaining and never criticises anyone. The other thing about her is that she only wears colourful clothes.

We're living under the dictatorship of black, and I have to admit I fall into line too often, probably out of laziness. Cosy proves it's possible to be elegant and colourful. She boldly bucks the trend to express her unique and joyful style. Colour is gaiety and light. In the sales, she'll snap up a bright green raincoat, a pair of yellow trousers, a Tyrian pink jumper or an indigo blue jacket, basically the things no one else buys. She says colour makes you glow, that it's her trick to looking cheerful, that you can see her from a long way off and don't forget her.

Colourful clothes aren't always a classy look, except when it comes to Cosy . . . and Queen Elizabeth.

What's in a young fifty-something's lingerie drawer?

At fifty, my mother was already wearing a girdle. She also had enormous knickers that must have reached up to her armpits and looked very strange to me. I saw these underpinnings hanging on the terrace, blowing in the wind, wondering if I would also have to subject my children, my husband or my lovers to things like that. Obviously, this was the sort of detail that made me think she can't have had many.

These days, a young fifty-something will sometimes still wear a thong, even if she finds it terribly uncomfortable – which in any case is the defining characteristic of a thong. So she only wears them in certain circumstances: for dancing, with white linen trousers or a figure-hugging sheath dress . . . Paradoxically, a thong only comes into its own when it can be seen, glimpsed or even better imagined, whereas the initial idea was to avoid any visible lines under your clothes, which between ourselves can also be achieved with quite high-waisted knickers a size bigger than normal.

As for bras, my mother's looked like tepees to my young eyes, but perhaps through a sort of augmented reality, everything looked much bigger to me. In any case, she wasn't as full-figured as her 'lingerie' might have suggested. These conical objects were more-or-less flesh coloured, in a combination of matt and shiny material that looked like wood. Mum, I'm sorry to be revealing the intimate details of your 'Cross your Hearts' – anyone born in the 1950s or 60s will understand, as will fans of Madonna or Jean-Paul Gaultier . . . I suppose the absence of variety was linked to the selection available back then in provincial shops.

So what do our bras look like these days?

First an observation: without the need for implants, we've grown a good bit in the space of a few years. Apart from sporty types, anorexics or those who've had the wind taken out of their sails by romantic or surgical ordeals, every woman over fifty finds herself going up a cup size, from A to B, or B to C. In a sense, few will complain and we (and our partners) see this physical change as an advantage.

My lingerie drawer reflects my whims and the rest of my wardrobe: it's ninety per cent composed of fabulous matching lacy sets with a built-in lack of comfort. The sort of thing we like (he likes) but isn't for wearing, at least during the day. They're reserved for special occasions. The remaining ten per cent is there to be worn and not seen. It's a bit like our brains. Apparently, we only use ten per cent of them. The rest is for decoration.

My regular underwear on a daily basis consists of cotton knickers with little flowers one size too big, which I 'match' with a moulded foam bra that keeps everything in line. The result: at fifty, boobs in good shape and no VPL.

Beauty

O genie of the lamp, let me be the first to find out about new developments in cosmetics, then other women may, but only much later.

At twenty, the main thing people notice is a fresh complexion and smoothness around the eyes. At fifty, your soul, your gaze, your charm and your wit become more important. Humour, kindness, cheerfulness, gentleness, intelligence and an ability to listen all have the power to 'smooth away' age, as well as being natural and free. At fifty, we have the face we deserve, resulting from a combination of our past history and present situation. Those who didn't manage to avoid sunshine and cigarettes have paid a high price, whilst the rest can congratulate themselves for protecting themselves and never taking up smoking.

Besides, I like to think that my skin looks a lot better than it would have if I hadn't spent the price of a studio flat in an up-and-coming area of Paris on cosmetics. But over time, I've calmed down a bit. Now my use of beauty creams is a matter of good sense, as far as I'm concerned. If you lubricate a dry surface (leather, for example), it's bound to make it more pliable. That's why I smother myself every day with creams that could almost be called ointments they're so thick and creamy. I slather and polish and will stick to you if you kiss me before ten in the morning, but I like to feel I'm well hydrated.

One day, I had a revelation. No, I know what you're thinking, I didn't discover the perfect substance with powers to repair, protect, plump, regenerate or fight the ageing process. At a certain point in my life, it simply became clear that I had to stop believing that the more a product cost, the more effective it would be. The high cost of a cosmetic is only justified if the bottle matches the tiles in your bathroom, or if the dreams it inspires can transport you far away.

My advice is to restrict yourself to the essentials: micellar water, make-up removal oil, a multi-purpose day and night cream, a total sunscreen over the top, a light body milk and a few accessories that you have to have in triplicate, like hair grips and tweezers, various sizes of brushes and nail scissors.

Compulsively purchasing cosmetics is a form of dreaming, and whilst dreams are not always effective, they are always indispensable. So I regularly go into a branch of Sephora and only come out two hours later, slathered, perfumed, powdered, happy to have fallen for products that appealed to me with their names, promises, smell, texture or packaging. I know, it's all just a paradox, but after all, why not.

You only need to have one magnifying mirror, because they're the most dreadful beauty accessories. Not because they're ugly but because they reveal truths you'd rather not know. If you're psychologically fragile, better to banish them from the bathroom, enough is enough. A magnifying mirror (minimum x7) is only feasible with the help of antidepressants or a strong stomach. But at the same time, don't put your head in the sand, if you get my drift. These gadgets can show you details that other people might spot first: blackheads, red marks, moles, blemishes, in-growing hairs . . .

But above all, the thing that haunts us fifty-somethings, drives us crazy, always comes back stronger, gets coarser over time, never stops growing and is only relieved by a scalpel or a laser beam is the rogue hair.

Luckily, in his infinite goodness, God also gave fifty-somethings the gift of incipient long-sightedness.

At fifty and beyond, just after 'How are you?' and 'What have you been up to?', 'Have you had something done?' is the third question you'll hear in the first five minutes when you meet up with a good friend for the first time in over six months, if she thinks you're looking well.

As with infidelity, admit nothing.

What was that? What? Oh no, not me, I've never done anything like that.

So it must be love then?

That must be it.

Bloody Le Doux, the friend must be thinking.

What you do is nobody else's business. Honestly.

But because this book is also a collection of confidences, I have to admit that in the not too distant past, I had a tiny little bit of work, almost nothing, just a symbolic trifle. Why did I feel I had to? Out of politeness, love, vanity, respect, a desire to make the best of myself, take your pick. I've always thought that if we have 'nothing' done, we run the risk of looking like our friends' grandmothers. So my recommendation has always been to have 'something' done, but only a little – excessive moderation, if you can grasp the significance of the oxymoron.

I'm the sort of person who might say as an opening gambit to her dermatologist, with the cattle prod poised over me (Le Doux sometimes thinks I exaggerate): 'Please can you make sure that no one will notice anything. I'll pay you, but I want you to do (almost) nothing. Make me think you're doing something, just inject me with some water, that'll be fine.' A crazy woman!

Avoid the pitfalls: never visit your dermatologist when you're depressed, and like the hairdresser, never give them free reign. In any case, free isn't the operative word here. I find it funny when some people follow our American friends in refering to aestheticians: which is trendier, more niche and more $$$. Dermatologist comes with a slight suggestion of acne, warts and psoriasis, whilst 'plastic surgeon' is only used by the practitioners themselves, and reeks of hospitals, scalpels and anaesthesia. No one says I'm going to see my plastic surgeon.

No matter where the action takes place, Le Doux won't countenance me having any kind of injection. He says it's obvious, it ages you, there's always a slight contrast with the neck or the hands, that it makes you look strange, and since nature and genetics have been fairly kind to me, we should leave things like that to actresses, the rich and the desperate. Too many injections are a sure sign you're in one of these three groups, and some cleverly combine a cocktail of all three.

The problem is good judgement. If you think you have a saggy eyelid, which may well only be visible to you, tell yourself it's just slackened enough to soften your look.

And that little line that wasn't there a few months ago, it's looking a bit deeper this morning. Perhaps, but what of it? Are you going to scrutinise your face like this every day? You might as well grab a whip and start flogging yourself.

I've already suggested you focus on other things with no sell-by date. Bear it in mind, and never forget that the gentleness of the soul has a way of showing itself in a person's face. Rather than emphasising the features, it softens them. It's true, age can sometimes also have this effect.

How to take care of yourself

Force yourself to hate the sun. At fifty – and so much the better if you adopted the habit from the age of thirty – never, ever, ever, ever go out in the sun without a total sunblock on your face, your neck and the backs of your hands. Not only in summer but all year round, in the shade as well, even in winter, perhaps even at night! The sun is wonderful, but our only choice is to give it up. No matter, we did enough sunbathing in the 1970s and 80s when our melanin stocks could still take it. We slathered ourselves in milking grease*, turned red and

---

* Translator's note: as the name suggests, the product was originally aimed at dairy farmers, but became popular as a low-cost tanning aid.

peeled like onions. Happily, fashions changed, and more importantly, the product was banned. Too late for some though, those who were born ten years earlier.

Sometimes, after a good night and a quiet day, with good make-up and in very low light, some kind souls who know the year I was born tell me I'm looking a few years younger. I take no notice, but I'm entitled to these flatteries, because past fifty, I know how quickly we lose our freshness after the slightest misdemeanour, alcohol, late night, summer excess or any other excess.

But still I hear them ask: 'So what's your secret? We know you often have a drink, sometimes smoke and never sleep?' At which point I give them my tips, depending on my latest discoveries. Every morning, I eat home-made granola (almonds, hazelnuts, a blend of cereal flakes, dried fruit, agave syrup, hazelnut oil, olive oil, coconut oil, ginger, nutmeg, salt, thirty minutes in the oven, stirring from time to time) with almond milk, then take a capsule of Spirulina (a form of algae with incredible properties). Twice a year, I take a course of iron and magnesium, and I never forget my little vial of vitamin D before winter. Besides that, I'm always trying new food supplements: the latest is marine collagen, which is supposed to be good for skin elasticity. I'll give you my verdict on its effects when they publish the sequel to this book. In general, I like to eat colourful foods: tomatoes, beetroots, blueberries, cranberries . . . which make me feel like I'm swallowing energy.

Finally and fundamentally, for good health and great skin, I can only advise combining exercise twice a day (make it quick) with sexual activity twice a week (take it slow). And at least once a day: have a good laugh, even though . . .

The drawbacks to laughter

Train yourself not to laugh unnecessarily: women who laugh too much, too often and too heartily have more wrinkles than serious types.

I know one fifty-something with the ability to simulate an affected laugh without moving her mouth. She emits a little chuckle that's quite charming (but a little weird) whilst holding a slightly limp hand against her motionless mouth. At the same time, she bends her neck and lowers her head so you can't see the corners of her mouth grow wider. She has no wrinkles, never goes out in the sun, has never touched a cigarette and has no man in her life.

Another of my friends, who's the same age, has smoked like a chimney all her life, laughs slightly hysterically at every opportunity (Le Doux finds it strange, I think it's endearing, and her laugh is fairly communicative), has spent her life in the sun, cares nothing for other people's opinions, and the only place she's being injected is in the bedroom (although he doesn't complain in certain circumstances, Le Doux does find me a touch vulgar at times).

Suffice it to say that my two friends are the same age, but one looks thirty years older than the other. I'm joking, of course, because there's nothing better than laughter, and it makes you happy. Between wrinkles and laughter, there's no contest. Even though I've sometimes spluttered to Le Doux: 'Stop making me laugh, you're shaking up my skin and loosening my collagen.'

Teething problems

In theory, our smile is something we can control.

In practice, our dentist will be the one to take care of it.

Be careful not to make any radical changes to your oral architecture: that break in the alignment is the little dental defect that shows that it's you, in the holistic sense of the term, and not a standardised clone designed to reassure the humanoids in front of you that you're not going to bite them. With a slight dental defect, what you lose in perfection, you make up for in personality.

Consider it an advantage and learn to love it. That slightly wonky canine is Cindy's beauty spot, Rossy's nose or the gap between Vanessa's teeth.

But if you like tea, coffee, red wine, cigarettes and blueberries, and you've never bothered to do the necessary, your teeth are bound to be the same shade of brown as a Vélib' bike. You can always learn to love your dark smile, or copy the gesture the friend I mentioned earlier uses to hide her mouth when she chuckles, but you could also brighten it up by half a shade (or why not a whole shade if you've got a lot of ground to make up), you'll only feel better for it.

Be careful not to go too far: steer clear of American-style optical white, or blue-looking teeth that make people drop their gaze ten centimetres when they're talking to you. Stay subtle. But slightly whiter teeth look clean, young and fresh!

Should you let your hair go grey?

White is for teeth, not hair.

The first white hair often appears in your mid-thirties. After angrily pulling it out, you realise that white hairs reproduce faster than the others. For every one you pull out, three more grow within a month. White hairs are thicker, with a different texture, and a peculiar look that's neither straight nor curly. They're both fundamentally and superficially distressing. With that first can of Diacolor, you're heading (no pun intended) for a process that will last thirty years. The natural, shiny hair of our youth will now be achieved with the help of various products that we put too much faith in. Oils, silicone and keratin masks promise a lot, but the results will never be perfect, and over the years, your hair will tend to get more and more frizzy. The only exceptions are natural straight-haired blondes and Asians. Who knows why everyone else is fated to live with ever fluffier hair. That said, if there's a chemical and statistical rule, it's that we become increasingly blonde over the years, which may have something to do with the sun's interaction with repeated applications of dye.

When it comes to hair I'm lucky to have inherited copious, thick hair like violin strings from my mother. But vigorous as it is, it still suffers the effects of time. And of course, there are two opposing schools of thought here. Those who accept their greying hair and the aging that comes with it, who no longer have to spend eighty euros every six weeks and risk giving themselves a thrombosis reading the celebrity gossip. And then there are the others, including myself. So it's either the hairdressers, or buying a kit for your roots at the supermarket for less than eight euros, an option that besides sparing you the need to sit in the hairdresser's window with khaki sludge on your head, only needs to be left in for ten minutes, so has the advantage of saving a substantial amount of time.

It's got nothing to do with the fear of getting old, it's just that covering up your grey hair is almost a form of personal hygiene. I'm not rushing headlong into this argument, because the Sophie Fontanel[*] effect has helped thousands of women rid themselves of their complexes and restored their pride in being themselves. I have no problem with this, if it helps them. I'm just worried about seeing women marching in the street, fists in the air, proud of whatever idiosyncrasy they've decided to embrace. Proud of their acne, their moustaches or their cellulite. 'Damn right, I've got yellow teeth, and I couldn't give a monkeys!'

Giving up on dyeing your grey hair can be understood or explained when it's linked to certain factors: budgetary, belief or preference.

In these cases, there's no debate.

Women in their fifties and women in general are increasingly embracing their grey hair. It's shows deter-

---

[*] Translator's note: a journalist and Instagram sensation known for her inventive style as well as her grey hair.

mination, guts and a good degree of boldness, almost like flicking the Vs. But at whom?

This choice has now become a symbol of self-affirmation, almost the trendy thing to do, and is in the process of putting hundreds of professional colourists out of work, even though the sector is immune to Uberisation. Few will contradict me when I say that whilst it's possible to dye your own hair, it's much more practical to have someone else do it.

For me, keeping my hair intact and natural would be difficult because it's only going white on the left-hand side. And I certainly don't want to be nicknamed Cruella. So no chance. In any case, it would feel like I was walking around naked or with a flashing sign strapped to my forehead: my identity card. A way of letting everyone you pass in the street know, if they hadn't noticed already, that you've reached that pivotal age when you throw in the towel.

When you stop covering up your grey hair, you stop trying to look younger, or not as old. People will tell you it's also about accepting your age. Yes, but in that case, where is the boundary between taking care of yourself and the imperious obsession of youth?

For my part, I place the cursor in the middle between taking care of yourself +++ and obsessing over your appearance − − −.

My mother 'gave up' at the age of eighty-two, when

she decided she'd had enough of dyes that made her head itch. For one of my friends, it was when she turned fifty and coincided with her coming out. For another friend, the desire to be natural translated into a poorly managed menopause accompanied by weight gain to irreversible levels. Tomorrow your weight, the next day it's your hair. A never-ending slippery slope.

Let your hair go grey, put on a pair of reading glasses, team a brown tweed skirt suit (with elasticated waist) with a pair of crêpe-soled moccasins and away you go, grandma! It's the perfect look for an appointment with an annuities expert.

This time will inevitably come. When it does, I'll stop buying women's magazines, hang up my high heels and save a fortune in cosmetics.

Comfort and practicality are the enemy cousins of gorgeous frivolity. We need to take care of ourselves because we're alive, because we'll like ourselves a little more, and if we add in some things that never go out of fashion like elegance and a smile, even better.

So what to do? Do you let your hair go grey or not?

Yes, if you're thirty-five.

Yes, if you have 200,000 followers on Instagram and you can turn your decision into a book, a success, make the nine o'clock news, and have enough money to compensate for the unwanted effects of age on your hair.

So yes.

But no!

Because fashionable or otherwise, salt and pepper hair will always equate to someone older.

I can hear the feminists rising up to a man to tell me: 'Hey, you're opening the door for the worst kind of chauvinism there. Start like that and you end up with fake breasts and duck lips. What's your game? And what about men, are they sexy with grey hair?'

I know, it's not fair that we find men charming with their baldness and silver hair. But things are changing, and I'm starting to see more and more of them at my hairdressers, hiding at the back of the salon, avoiding your eyes with dye on their temples. The scene always makes me want to smile, take a quick picture and post it on Instagram (something I've not yet dared to do).

But why can't I help making a personal judgement on this still rare male behaviour? Why do I think that dyeing your hair is part and parcel of looking after yourself for a woman, but tends to make a man look less masculine? At least in my eyes. Why do we think it's normal that we have to make these efforts?

Like many women of my generation, I feel I'm not yet ready to pursue the feminist revolution led with beating drums by young forty-somethings. My superego is stronger, my upbringing too well-rooted, too Mediterranean. Am I the victim of thought patterns that have left me a dyed in the wool believer that women have to fight to stay thin, young, beautiful and sexy whilst men's most important role is to exude the power to protect us? I admire the trailblazers. I'm counting on them, and on you millennials out there, to shake up the archetypes of seduction, to change our perceptions, judgements and desires.

How can we convince the world around us in general and women's media in particular to update the rules of beauty and standards of sexiness? I sometimes want to scream at the pages of our magazines, when they persist in presenting images of women at the limits of their dignity. My favourite magazine, the one I've read since I learnt to read, has a girl on its cover with a slightly dumb expression, mouth half-open, in a provocative pose, with bare thighs. Why? Those who claim to speak for us should be fighting to change the paradigms of women's roles and behaviour.

Weight restriction

O genie of the lamp, let food have no effect on me.

When the time comes to give up, we'll shout from the rooftops that there will be no more expensive makeovers and weighing ourselves twice a day, whilst previously prohibited treats like pastries for supper, fizzy drinks or salt and vinegar crisps at aperitif time will be back on the menu. Finally rid of bodily concerns, we will simply become thinking reeds* on the slippery slope of unrepressed appetite and indifference to matters of seduction. We will let ourselves peacefully expand with the provocative smile of those who are no longer concerned about love handles, cellulite and sagging orange-peel skin. Retiring from the game of love will allow us this freedom.

But before reaching that point, the young fifty-something will fight relentlessly to keep in shape and maintain an appetite for food, which is never far from the desire to be loved.

A few random thoughts on weight:

Gain weight and you risk losing confidence.

A little extra weight ages you a lot.

Weight is like temperature. There's the weight you are and the weight you feel.

At any given weight, having friends who are fatter than you makes you happy, whereas having thinner friends

---

* Translator's note: In Blaise Pascal's *Thoughts*, humans are described as 'thinking reeds' to contrast our physical weakness compared to the universe with the nobility we gain through our ability to think.

definitely contributes to depression. Women don't dream of meeting Prince Charming, their greatest dream is to eat without putting on weight. Something you boast about before turning fifty, and always long for afterwards, in vain.

At twenty, you get fat by eating fast food, at thirty, by eating pasta, at forty by eating an apple, at fifty by drinking water, and at sixty, breathing makes you fat. Weight has a life of its own, something mathematical, exponential, inevitable. So keeping your eye on the scales and a hand on your weight is always desirable, a part of looking after yourself that goes with dyeing your roots and size ten trousers.

Without special attention on an almost day basis and an exercise regime worthy of the name, the union rate after fifty is at least an extra half a kilo a year. Later, your weight will stabilise, but when the 'afterwards' body shape sets in for good, it's too late. The kilos are there to stay. Of course, it's not too serious. Changing your wardrobe is only ever a financial issue, but nonetheless, adopting a new image and getting used to a new silhouette whilst keeping a smile on your face is not so easy.

So with the exception of a few women with pituitary gland issues, we're all more or less on a diet after fifty, and those who aren't but still manage to stay thin should keep it to themselves.

The upshot is that there is only one definitive mental solution: never drop your guard. And at the same time, live well and enjoy the good things in life. So how can we satisfy our appetites without the skin on our faces ageing at the speed of light?

Losing a few kilos is possible, but putting them on is so much easier! There are solutions, diets and strategies. To each her own. Mine is to stuff myself with things that don't make you fat and are full of water. The feeling of fullness is immediate, and even if it doesn't last, it will help you get by until the next meal.

So what's the advantage of slimming?

Feeling lighter, which has an effect on your mood.

Having more endurance for running or your dance class.

Being able to fit into the trousers you bought a size too small in anticipation of this moment.

Being able to tuck in again.

Good health!

Health issues specific to people in their fifties are numerous, and creep up on you.

You realise your age the day you receive a circular offering you a free colorectal examination, rather than a voucher sent by the local hairdresser inviting you to sample her skills as a colourist. Just a simple check on your internal pipework. A little camera with a homing device will go and take a look at your innards, and record a video that won't necessarily show you in your best light, although everything should remain confidential between you and the gentleman who now knows your back passage like the back of his hand.

On a more feminine note, you have the mammogram to look forward to. The breast (slice of ham) is placed between two metal places (slices of bread) which will squeeze until they form a sandwich. At which point, you'll hold your breath just long enough for a quick dose of allegedly carcinogenic rays. After a vertical then a horizontal sandwich, you'll be presented with some indecisive results. With a deceptively reassuring dubious look, they'll encourage you to come back next year.

Happily, it's not all this bad, and one of the advantages of being in our fifties is the knowledge we have of our bodies. At this point, we know when to self-medicate and at what dose. We can tell the difference between drinking too much fruit juice and gastroenteritis or between a urinary tract infection and a yeast infection. Those who've experienced both or all four will know what I'm talking about.

My secret elixir of youth

There are some words that must never be spoken. Except for a rhyme, a joke or in extreme medical circumstances. In fact, those words aren't even part of my vocabulary. Nevertheless, trying to write a book about young fifty-somethings without mentioning the 'menopause' even once would be a denial by omission. A bit like talking about love without mentioning sex.

I remember my mother suddenly running with sweat; in the space of a few seconds, it looked like she'd come out of the shower fully dressed. Hot flushes are the first sign, followed by various issues. Things can then go very quickly, depending on your individual metabolism.

Luckily, Zorro has come to the rescue.

A squirt on the arm in the morning, a pill like a Tic-Tac in the evening, and the problem is solved: mood calmed, weight stabilised and heading down, sleeping patterns restored, hot flushes eradicated, libido reactivated.

People see today's fifty-somethings as a new phenomenon in society, amazed at how little they have in common with those of the previous generation. That they're staying thinner and younger for longer, that their skin is less wrinkled, their hair is thicker and they're overflowing with sexual energy.

And why is that, do you think?

Better diet?

Better living standards?

Food supplements?

Not necessarily. There may be something more. No, what's new is that we now know how to solve the problem. When a woman is fifty going on fifteen and we try to analyse the whys and the wherefores, you can be sure she's on hormone replacement therapy.

Unless there are medical reasons, you're morally opposed to medication or you live in the back of beyond with an ancient husband who no longer takes much advantage of you, my advice is that it would be a shame to deprive yourself. Because as well as tangibly improving your everyday quality of life, the treatment also apparently has preventative benefits for your bone and cardio-vascular health.

I'm not being paid by a pharmaceutical company for writing this.

As I write these lines, I'm in a house out in the wilds of Corsican *maquis*, where my host has very tactfully warned us that we shouldn't put 'things' down the toilets, because despite the modern facilities, these septic tanks can't cope with everything. He mentions cotton buds, packaging and so on.

I wait for him to call a spade a spade. But no. With a

caustic smile, I would have reassured him, whilst adding that I would have loved to have chucked a tampon in his tank.

Frozen shoulder: a shocking story

Or how a slightly more vigorous exercise class than usual can lead to months of physiotherapy and pain. I'd never heard of a frozen shoulder until I got one. It's like devil setting up shop in your shoulder and only coming out two years later. All because you went a bit overboard with your sun salutation or decided to do some press-ups after a quiet jog.

There are several ways to solve a medical issue. There's the classic method, where a medical practitioner weighs up the situation and sometimes prescribes some drugs. Then there's Dr Li's method, which is a form of legalised torture. His patients can't be aware that his acupuncture could be a threat to their dignity.

When my condition was diagnosed, I went straight to the internet medical forums in search of hope and solutions. All I found were people resigned to their fate with just two watchwords: suffering and patience. The very things I can't stand. Frozen shoulder is a nasty little condition that threatens fifty-somethings in general and women in particular. In France, I'd already seen a rheumatologist, an osteopath, a physio, a homeopath, an acupuncturist, a masseur, a masseuse, and had even visited a magnetic healer. None of them had been able to tame the beast. Two failed injections down the line, exhausted by the persistent pain, discouraged by the ineffectiveness of the solutions I was offered, and tired of fighting, I made an appointment on arrival on holiday in New York with the umpteenth allegedly 'miracle-working' acupuncturist, whose skills had been insistently recommended by one of my friends.

The day of the appointment, I arrived arm in arm with my frozen shoulder in a sort of kitsch-y, dusty place from another era in the heart of Wall Street. Before meeting the good doctor, I filled in an extremely intrusive medical questionnaire, and in the usual American style, signed a four-page contract promising that even if I died, Dr Li would be utterly blameless. This last point is important, because it must be this administrative safety net that allows Dr Li the peace of mind to practise a form of therapy with no references to back it up, with an approach that is much more homespun than academically trained.

I'm thankful to be living in a time of peace, because I admit that I'd confess to anything under torture: huge needles stuck into knotted muscles (howls), muscles zapped with pulses of electricity controlled by a knob that Li

kept turning further to the right to measure my resistance
(screams), vigorous massage with the thumb (whimpers),
suction cups on the skin (staccato yells). Annoyed by
these outbursts of acute sensitivity, he stuck a towel in my
mouth to stop me from shouting, or at least to make sure
the sound was muffled. So as not to alarm the patients in
the waiting room (or should I say holding pen?).

I left Li's surgery tattooed Maori-style with aubergine-
coloured circles, certain I wasn't enough of a masochist
to go back and put my already bruised shoulder through
any more assaults.

I'll never know what was most effective in calming
the pain that had tyrannised my days and my nights,
the dreadful torture Dr Li inflicted with his 'special
needles', or the herbal infusions tasting of compost that
he made me swallow twice a day. The fact is that this first
appointment put an end to two long months of agony
and insomnia. For ages, I hadn't been able to swing my
arms in a circle, but from the very next day, I was able
to type on my Mac and pick up a cup without any pain.

Bruises

The standard-issue tattoo for a fifty-something isn't the
salamander on the shoulder favoured by young New-

Yorkers. We've gone beyond the age of having indelible designs drawn on our skin. The passage of time is already doing enough, and there's no need to draw attention to our sagging flesh.

No, in your fifties, rather than tattoos, you have bruises!

When a fifty-something bumps into something, the dreaded mark makes its appearance, growing, turning blue and spreading beneath her delicate white skin. A fifty-something's bruise is longer-lasting and grows darker and darker on the Pantone scale, ranging from dark purple to aniseed yellow. It only disappears after many weeks, becoming a trademark, a certificate of traceability. So after fifty, take the haemophiliac approach, at least in summer, or barricade yourself behind a suit of armour or a protective harness: padded trousers, elbow guards, shin pads, knee pads . . . Or go to town with the Arnica, in pills, homeopathic remedies, gels and creams.

Protect yourself from bumps, corners lurk at every turn,
Low tables get you on the calf, you know you'll never learn,
Then taller tables lie in wait for tender upper thighs,
Not to mention careless knees, it brings tears to the eyes.

Every piece of furniture presents a spiky threat,
Running to the dining room is something you'll regret.
These bruises grow familiar,
Corresponding to my furniture,
The classic chair in stainless steel,
With corners that the shins will feel,
Armrests that attack as soon as they're able
A bruise just as chic as your Noguchi table.
Even rounded edges do nothing to protect us,
The thick glass top will never stop it trying to molest us.
I can't complain, it's not their fault, the clumsiness is
*   mine,*
If I could only stand up straight then it would be just
*   fine.*
Please excuse this small digression,
Poetry is my obsession.

'That's great! So now the bruise is your muse,' says
Le Doux.

Ah Le Doux! Always ready with a quip.

Dizziness

Paris, last Sunday, 10 a.m . . .

   All of a sudden, I felt dizzy. I lost my balance and

felt myself starting to go, but found the strength to drag myself to bed. Lying on my back, blurry-eyed, I watched the ceiling spinning round at speed. Then it started to get worse, the pins and needles in my fingers spreading by the second. An outside force had taken control of my body and was making the decisions.

The ambulance took me to the emergency department at Lariboisière hospital, accompanied by Le Doux, who was beside himself. I'll spare you the details: the interminable wait on my trolley next to an apprentice terrorist who was in a bad way but still guarded by a dozen policemen armed to the teeth; having to repeat what had happened thirty times to different people . . . Then doctors, clinical tests and back home with an appointment for the next day, the day after that, and the day after that.

The story could have ended there, and you would have found a discreet note on my blog and my Facebook wall written by one of my children to say that my account was closed, and my literary hijinks were over.

But since it turned out well this time, I'd like to take the opportunity to remind everyone that I'm not donating my body to science and my credit card codes are in the left-hand pocket of my Balenciaga jacket, a fact that could come in useful in an emergency to cover the unexpected incidental expenses (petits fours, floral decorations, a little something for the choirboys . . .) that crop up after this sort of domestic drama.

Do you know what? It can happen to anyone. One day, splat, you land head first in your plate. Goodnight, Vienna!

On what could have been my last morning, I instantly found my head was filled with the most random thoughts: have I waxed properly?; damn it, everyone's going to find out how old I really am; did I put on a matching bra and knickers this morning; no, I don't want to miss the release of *Would I Lie to You 4*, nor waste my plane ticket for New York next week . . .

Still so many things to see and people to disappoint, and I'd promised to finish writing this book by the end of the year.

The lesson: an awareness that the best days are still ahead of me.

The diagnosis: vestibular neuritis, nothing very serious, just very scary.

Cigarettes and other drugs

At fifty, you need to have given up smoking, even if you tell yourself you'll take it up again later on, much later on, when your skin, other people's opinions and even your health are unimportant. I like the act of smoking, the faint burning sound when you take a drag, and the convivial contact with other people. We've yet to discover a better way to start chatting someone up than 'Could you spare a cigarette?' I sometimes smoke after dinner. I like to hold a cigarette between my fingers, take a first drag and put it out quickly. As with any other addictive product, I try to keep control and enjoy keeping out of its clutches, thinking to myself, with a certain arrogance, 'Oh no, you won't get me, my dear.'

Which is lucky, because smoking puts years on your face and takes years off your life expectancy. We're all equal when it comes to cigarettes, which leave us with a rasping voice, withered skin, diseases by the shovel load and breath that could fell an ox at twenty paces. But when they have us in their grasp, they become our most faithful friends. Sometimes till death us do part!

I've also been able to keep away from drugs, having been too busy building my professional skills and reputation. These days, my work can accommodate things that can no longer damage my reputation – at my age, it's been made, supposing I have one.

But even so, before my time is up, I'd like to try cocaine at least once.

Should you share recommendations?

As fifty-somethings, we're people of high standards and refined tastes, and for each type of business in our neighbourhood, we know who's 'very good' or even 'the best'. The best cheesemonger, the best butcher, the best organic market ... and modestly or evangelically, we enjoy sharing our tips with our friends, following the principle that 'my friend's butchers are my butchers'.

But when it comes to passing on the addresses of people who trade on their skills – dentists (for implants), dermatologists (for injections) or osteopaths (for the snap, crackle and pop) – experience proves that it's best to keep your contacts to yourself. So when someone asks, 'You don't happen to know a good dentist, do you?', if you want to avoid complications and keep your friends, reply with a simple 'No, sorry'. Because if one of your friends unfortunately had a bad experience, as can happen, it would be bound to be your fault.

Imagine if the wonderful dermatologist who normally wields a needle like a goldsmith and has worked miracles on you (temporary miracles, because as you know, the effects of those injections never last) managed to hit your friend's optical nerve. She begged you to give her the contact details, but now she's left with a funny lopsided look with one eye wide open and is baying for your blood.

Similarly, keep your accountant to yourself, just in case he liquidates her investments, your osteopath in case he pops a disc in her neck, and your lawyer, who will inevitably ensure her divorce proceedings drag on for years.

All right, so no one's going to slip you the name of a good proctologist. If things went wrong, it would be a real bummer . . . (OK, I won't put that one in, I tell Le Doux, promising to publish the book under a pseudonym.)

In general, you're better off not praising anyone's talents, there's nothing in it for you. Beside the danger of losing friends if it goes wrong, you run the risk of causing price inflation and making it harder to get an appointment for yourself.

A good gynaecologist? Sorry, no.

But I know a good butcher.

Time to exercise

O genie of the oil lamp, may my joints always be sufficiently lubricated.

Despite our chronic youthfulness, we're forced to admit that there are sports for the young and sports for older people. There are no obligations, but everything is expected. Just like we have to eat our five a day, we believe them when they say that we have to do regular physical exercise. And make time for the ideal activity. And feel guilty because we're never as good as the media say we should be. So what are the physical activities that offer the best ratio of effort to results and clear conscience?

At fifty, how do you keep in shape without beating yourself up?

Over the years, I've gradually become aware of the fragility of my skeleton and the prolonged discomfort that inevitably results when I push myself: soreness in the lower back, tight muscles, unexpected cramps . . . Lumbago, tendonitis, sprains or a cricked neck are never too far away. Each time I overdo it, I pay an increasingly heavy price. And yet I can't help regularly checking if my body will cope with the demands I make, hoping (in vain) that it will respond like it used to. It's fine to tag along with the youngsters for some climbing, archery or interval running, just don't cross the line between 'beneficial exercise' and 'going beyond your limits'. Efforts are always rewarded, of course, and regular physical activity makes you feel like you're keeping up the pace. So you think that you can't regress.

Mistake! Each day of physical inactivity will make it even more painful to restart. You have to constantly fire yourself up, and there are new enemies to deal with: a heart that's not what it once was, rust encroaching on the joints, disproportionate consequences when you get injured and the growing laziness that encourages us at some point to consider Churchill's attitude to sport. Everyone needs to find the physical activity that suits them best. Between frenetic Zumba and qigong for the mind, the choice is vast.

Run, run, run

I've been going running ever since I was too old for it. Before, in my twenties and thirties, when running wasn't as fashionable as it is now, I preferred dancing or swimming.

Nowadays, once or sometimes twice a week I pull on some leggings, hop on my bike and head to the park. My trainer is Le Doux, and I try to conceal my immense laziness from him as best I can. I never feel like running: the before is the bit I can't stand, whereas I much prefer the after. It's a struggle to set off on the first lap, feeling so heavy it's as if I'm carrying sacks of water on my back. By the end of the third lap, I think about my endorphins waking up and the feeling of well-being that will flood through me at the end of the run. For a few seconds, in these moments of bodily and hormonal joy, I feel really great. The only thing that takes you to the same place is good sex.

I'm always pleased to have gone running, especially because those are the days when I treat myself to a pure butter croissant afterwards, sometimes two. A guilt-free reward that nevertheless cancels out some of my efforts.

Striding into the distance

I've read that walking with long strides is very productive. A long, fast walk, they say, is almost better than a short run. Oh really? Better for what? For the joints, very probably. For the heart? Possibly. It all depends on how long you spend exercising. Some also point out that fast walking is an eco-friendly, accessible and communal activity. I always like to be taken on walks, quite challenging ones where you climb up amongst the scree and the pine trees. I'll gaze off into the distance beyond the clouds and breathe in the purer air as I enjoy the silence, with nothing but the sounds of nature to be heard. For inspiration, I'll imagine I'm a mountain goat. Later, after several hours of inner calm in the natural world, I'll do simple things: sit on a tree trunk, slice up a sausage and have a little drink.

Yoga? And dancing?

I'm one of those people who've parted company with yoga. I loved it so much, then grew weary, particularly my body. I know that almost everyone disagrees with me, seeing yoga as something untouchable that cannot be criticised because it does so many people so much good. But that's the way it is. I don't want to do any more yoga. All the different varieties: Bikram, Iyengar, Vinyasa, Ashtanga, Hatha . . . All the variations – yoga for sex, yoga for the eyes, yoga for the hormones, laughter yoga, yoga recipes – it all only amused me for so long. Still, I spent ten years convincing myself I liked it. Whereas apart from the quiet sessions of relaxation and breathing – and even those were only effective the day after a late night, when my head would nod to the sound of the teacher's hypnotic OM – all the rest really wasn't for me. Exhilaration and joy are the only things that truly relax me. I had to admit that not only was yoga not doing me good, it was doing the opposite.

The poses weren't invented for a physiology like mine. Twisting myself in unnatural ways is just painful, breathing from the stomach bores me and I don't understand Sanskrit. The exoticism that goes with it isn't enough to contradict the evidence that I'm wasting my time.

When I stopped yoga, I also cancelled my season ticket with the osteopath. 'It's because you had a bad teacher,' I can hear you all saying with one voice. The main problem is that I'm a poor student with limited abilities. I prefer the more Western feel of Pilates, and its chest breathing seems more natural to me. No fuss, no Indian-sounding words, just one movement, then two, then three, in succession, and never the same one twice.

But what inspires me and does me the power of good is dancing. I love to dance. In the evenings, when the children aren't there (and even when they are), Le Doux and I dance. At my signal, he puts on his latest sonic obsession, and in a flash, we're on our feet on the living room carpet. Two harmless but crazy fifty-somethings dancing like mad things. The fun lasts about ten minutes, then I collapse, gasping for breath, my heart pounding and dying for a drink. 'It's my lungs,' I say to Le Doux between two gulps of ice-cold Chardonnay. That's why I struggle to get through a ninety-minute modern jazz lesson. It's because I'm short of breath. I rediscovered dance in my fifties, when I happened to find myself living a few metres away from a dance centre. Since then, I've been doing ballet fitness, jazz or classical dance every week. I put on my pumps and black tights and join the girls with their hair in buns who hold their heads straight and high, as if there was an invisible wire attaching them to the ceiling. Being surrounded by these young women in leotards does me good. Apart from the multiple mirrors that correct your posture with a cruel and eagle-eyed precision, which I avoid looking in, I'm one of them. But my skeleton persists in not responding to the same cues as it used to. It's a difficult thing to admit, and I think I'm happy to be in complete denial of my subtle degeneration – you know, it's strange, before I could do the box splits, but now I'm all rust and bone. So I put my body on one axis and my brain on the other, and the brain refuses to back down

Sometimes I lie in bed with my eyes closed and imagine myself sprinting through my run-up, then performing a twisting triple summersault with a perfect landing. Vestigial memories of the 1976 Olympic Games. My name is Nadia.

Work and money: thriving on less

Over fifty: the end of the steady job

For women, after fifty, the world of work is no longer stretching out its hand, the most you can hope for is a finger . . . the middle one.

You're an employee sitting in a safe little cupboard, with a computer, a desk, an NYC mug and a swivel chair. As long as the company is in the black, you'll be safe, happy and warm. Except that one day, there's a rumour in the corridors that you're being outperformed by your main competitor, that your boss has sold out, there's going to be a merger, it's crisis time and there's a nasty plan in the works. This is when the details of a specialist lawyer would come in very handy.

Negotiate your exit before you get caught out. It's the same as matters of the heart. When things start to smell of ripe pâté, heavy reproaches and prolonged silences, it's best to understand what's going on, hear the explanations, and if need be, prepare your escape route. Evaluate the seriousness of the situation and avoid going into denial, which will just lead to more and more lumps in the throat. The quicker you leave, the quicker you can move on to something else. So leave the company, guilt-free, with a cheque in your pocket, and a training plan negotiated by your lawyer. Of course, this is easy to say or to write, but it's not easy to face the fears that are triggered like airbags as soon as the prospect of change rears its head.

Leaving home, moving house, moving in together, getting divorced, moving again, being made redundant . . . the fear always comes before, sometimes during. Afterwards, generally, you congratulate yourself for your bravery and stylish handling of these difficult times. Above all, please don't despair, don't go thinking 'I'll get depressed if I stop working.' Instead, tell yourself that now's the time, you need to reinvent yourself, and every risk is an opportunity. Rest assured that the end of one era is the beginning of the next, and that the new era will be an interesting one. Send out a few messages to your entourage, a knock on the door to send your regards to your network. All these little pebbles on the floor will lead you somewhere. Don't rush. One day, as if it was staring you in the face, you'll say to yourself: OK, I've found my niche. Someone you meet, a proposal, an opportunity. Keep your eyes open and it will come, I promise you.

A shocking story

When her company came under new ownership, one of my friends who worked as director of communications suddenly found herself pushed towards the exit. After receiving a slightly insulting financial proposal, she instructed a lawyer and tried to defend herself. It was a bitter struggle, but happily, during this period of instability, she was contacted by a major recruitment firm about a similar job at a prestigious company.

A miracle! She was in the wrong half of her fifties and starting to despair, but the news put a bit of a spring back in her step. As the proposal became clearer, she decided to ease up on the other lot. Her lawyer didn't really agree, and advised her to attack.

'You're on the shortlist and very well placed,' she was told by the headhunters. 'Come in tomorrow for a final interview.' The implication being that it was almost a formality. She was over the moon. Naturally, she told herself that as she'd almost got this new job, given that the business world isn't that big, and she had a reasonably high profile, it wasn't ideal for people to know that she was taking the company making her redundant to an industrial tribunal. So she decided to give up on her legal battle and accept the slim pickings.

The day after she signed the agreement with her company, the headhunter told her that in the end she hadn't been selected. Of course, no one will ever be able to prove that the headhunter was in cahoots with the company. But when she told me that she'd been called out of the blue before she'd accepted the settlement agreement, I couldn't help being convinced that it had been a trap.

The job market is so cruel to a fifty-something who's been left by the wayside. At the time, she was in despair. And then, on the edge of the abyss, she spread out her arms and took a leap into the void. She's happy now, making wooden cabins in the forest.

The moral of the story is that when you're made redundant at over fifty-five, don't try to look for an equivalent job, you won't find one. If you don't have the soul of an entrepreneur, blame your parents, your genes or whatever you like, but in order to find a job with a new company, it's the same as the dating game, you'll have to lower your expectations.

When it comes to love, you'll find it easier to meet a man with some minor defects: challenging looks, restricted interests, finances in a mess, bus pass, dodgy prostate . . . On the job front, there's a likelihood it will be less well-paid and less interesting, provided you're offered one at all. Your CV may have looked good in the 1990s but it's not much use now, except as a record of professional achievements that all happened a long time ago . . . and to reveal your age. You won't have mentioned it, of course, but given the extent of your experience, the recruiter will go straight to the date you graduated from university, make a quick calculation, and in the absence of a ministerial recommendation (at the very least!), boom, dustbin. Sending out your CV only makes sense before fifty. After that, you'll need to cosy up to your address book, if you were sensible enough to keep it up to date.

But perhaps your biggest champion (the minister himself) instructed the headhunter to see you. He'll receive a pompous yet syrupy standard letter on embossed paper, pre-written by a civil service secretary, singing the praises of your exceptional qualities, legendary propriety and past successes.

And then in an air-conditioned glass office, you'll find yourself in front of a thirty-year-old in shoes with tassels on them, who, with unrestrained arrogance, will read your employment history out loud to you, as if it was in Finnish: 'Kraft', 'PPR', 'Manufrance', 'Saint-Gobain-Pont-à-Mousson'. Then he'll stop, raise an eyebrow and ask you, 'So what exactly do these companies do?'

The mere fact of having to answer him will make you want to throw up.

You'll be talking about a different era, he'll use horrible terminology you don't understand. In an age of Newspeak and the tyranny of Anglicisms ending in 'ing', such as wording, outsourcing and coding, you'll struggle to present your skills in the appropriate way. Turn your attention to other centres of interest and look elsewhere. Forget about tossers in tasselled shoes.

The reinvention is underway!

Your own, right now.

What to do next

I've worked hard over the course of my life, but only between the third term of my last year at school and the age of forty-eight. In other words, thirty years in all, to the day. Before that, I was an almost autistic child, a stammering schoolgirl, a struggling primary school pupil and a wretched high school student.

One day, due to a moment of rage (thanks, Dad) combined with inspiration and destiny's sprinkling of good fortune, I flew the nest and kept my nose to the grindstone for three decades. Leaving home was my personal revolution, but the relentless work was definitely my father's programming.

You see my father brainlessly worshipped work, with the aim of amassing a legacy that would be enough to make sense of his life. But money, which is what drives most people in their careers, was only a side issue for him, at best a diversion. Money was to be earned, not spent. You watched it come in, never leave. Sometimes, my father got up at night to do the accounts, then went back to bed, satisfied. As for my mother, she was a housewife, but the role didn't suit her. She dreamed of escape, although she'd never had a bank card, a driving licence or a confirmed lover. The rituals were planted like stakes in her timetable. The day was structured according to an age-old rhythm that no one would have dreamt of challenging, least of all her. Meals, housework, shopping, a bit of gossip and the annual bottle of Guerlain formed the sum total of her life. She said she had a lot of work. It must have been true, at least in the way she understood it. But as she never received any financial reward, the notion of work according to the maternal model was never an activity I wanted to associate myself with. So it was thanks to the paternal model, the very one I was running away from, that I was able to build a life for myself and earn my hard-fought living.

Breaking away from your parents is the best experience there is. The satisfaction that comes from what you've achieved yourself is immense. But some parents are more difficult to leave than others: too much love, too many ties, too many wings deliberately clipped. So thank you to mine for having equipped me for independence, but also for providing me with numerous good reasons to leave them, and as many to love them.

But before I turned fifty, I decided to stop working. In twenty years, the advertising market had changed, and so had I. I'd done the rounds of my speciality several times, and the tricks we used to entice the consumer had begun to seem less and less ethical. Behind my ear, a little voice was begging me to stop wasting my life for profit. I couldn't see what I could possibly gain from more time spent in meetings and managing projects. More money? Certainly. But the price tag on my boredom and my freedom was higher still. So I found an emergency exit and used it.

I was out.

At that point, everyone said: 'Are you crazy, what are you going to do now?'

I can talk about the most alienating and destructive aspects of work, but I feel I'm even better placed to talk about not working and the fear of the void we inevitably feel when people ask: 'So what are you doing now?'

For years, I'd become accustomed to saying 'I run an advertising agency' and enjoying the after-effect. Overnight, I had to switch to the past tense. At first, I always talked about what I'd done before and forgot about the present. Then one day, I ended up embracing it: 'I don't work.' This answer was generally followed by a long pause and a slight embarrassment, somewhere between modesty and provocation.

Thanks to my situation, I've been able to enjoy the ambiguous responses given by vaguely inactive people who are used to this question, which often begin with 'at the moment . . .' 'I work for a foundation' demands respect, but mainly means you've got connections and time on your hands. 'I'm in tourism' can mean you rent out your apartment on Airbnb and you're there to greet your guests. 'I'm involved with a start-up' means that you've lent a friend some money and are giving them a helping hand. 'I'm a partner in a small business' doesn't necessarily mean you're playing an active role. 'I'm between two jobs' is a polite way of saying you've been fired and you're looking for something else.

Evasiveness can attract attention and curiosity, so you can dodge the question by replying with something like: 'Right now, I'm enjoying a plate of chicken with ratatouille.' And then there are expressions that can never be used, on pain of immediate social death: 'I'm unemployed' or 'I'm retired.'

At fifty, we haven't got to that point yet, although in some companies in France, you can take advantage of your retirement rights earlier under certain circumstances, for example if you've had three children. Then take off the notice period, paid holidays, add in a little bit of low-level sick leave, and you're free from your employer at fifty-six.

You'll very quickly learn to decode the truth hiding behind the slightly vague descriptions of the most exuberant artistic creativity: non-figurative painting, barbed-wire sculpture, liturgical dance, plant decoration, 'Indian trading', or door to door selling of various trinkets picked up at a night market in Goa. Behind this smokescreen, there's often a little nest egg hidden under the pillow, from a source they like to keep quiet: a corporate redundancy plan, unexpected inheritance, rental income, compensatory divorce payment, understanding husband, patron with a court-appointed guardian . . . 'I'm in contemporary art', is another thing I sometimes hear. This is a sector that provides the world's great reservoir of activity for the idle rich, and is frequently inhabited by beautiful, ambiguously wealthy women, whose fortunes owe more to their marriages or being born with oral silverware than their artistic knowledge and judgement.

Be sure to tell yourself that 'I don't do anything' is not an option. Even those who haven't got the time to do anything do something. You only say "I'm not doing anything" to protest your innocence. Also be aware that there are sanctified responses that will almost have people bowing down in front of you. 'I write', for example, will get you close to the centre of the table. 'I've been published' will get you a seat at the host's right hand, provided of course you don't live in the fifth, sixth or seventh arrondissement in Paris, where EVERYONE writes.

So you don't have an official occupation? Depending on who you're talking to, you'll be put at the back, in a corner, at the end of the table, facing backwards, upside down, filtered out, muted ... But the response might just as easily be: 'Nothing? That's wonderful!' In most cases, it will be heartfelt, in some cases polite, or perhaps it will come with a pinch of jealousy, particularly if you're talking to someone who spends two hours a day on public transport and endures the erratic behaviour of a perverse, tyrannical boss.

I really liked the unapologetic line I heard from a pretty fifty-something at one of those dinners on the Rive Gauche where everything seems easy and charming. Her reply was: 'I don't do anything, but I do it well.' This little musical adage with its accompanying innocent smile went down a storm. One to remember, I told myself, but only if the décor and the environment are appropriate. Ideally, you'll have several possible answers and serve up the one that's most appropriate to the nosy parker in question. I have plenty in stock in my personal warehouse, ranging from the utter lie to the 'slightly true'.

I also think about all those jobs that don't always provide the rapid return on investment we hope for, and take time and money simply to be able to get started. Discovering painting in the second half of your life is often one of these. You have to buy materials, set aside a room in your apartment to work in, or maybe hire a studio, send out invitations to the private view, pay the gallery that exhibits your work, and shell out for the sparkling wine. After that, everything will depend on the quality of your work and your address book.

Getting on well with people, having wealthy contacts and a name that sells and sounds the part are the three necessities for transforming yourself into a 'late-blooming artist'. With a short training course, you can become a florist, a bookbinder, or better still a whole host of impressive-sounding jobs ending in '-pist', '-path' or '-gist'. Your investment costs will be low (a place to work, a gold plaque and four screws), but you'll still have to publicise yourself (personal network, the services of a community manager) and demonstrate some proven experience or a particular gift.

But the category most popular amongst fifty-somethings is undoubtedly 'coach'. After fifty, French woman become coaches. A coach is the '-pist', '-path' and '-gist' rolled into one. When it comes with the words 'sports', it's clearly a synonym for trainer, but when the business card reads 'life coach', the field of expertise is a little hazier.

I would certainly never set out to undermine the occupation. It's just there are so many of them!

'I've gone back to studying' will limit the damage and keep up appearances. But everyone knows you don't start studying after fifty unless you've lost your job. Instead, try 'I've become a student again'. It means the same thing but has a young feel to it. It's also a way to start a conversation (or end one).

'Ah, a masters in African literature!'

'Great!'

A return to academic life is something that could be considered in redundancy negotiations. And why not at one of the prestigious universities? So although your CV is a label of identity that will no longer be of any use to you in the final straight of your professional career, it will acquire the halo of a prestigious master's degree that will immediately eclipse any other qualifications. Your commercial vocational diploma, your university general studies diploma in Spanish, your degree in psychomotor therapy, all forgotten. The big names in higher education trade on their image and are well aware that these unemployed executives who will be back on the job market as soon as their course is over are a financial godsend. After all your efforts, there won't necessarily be a job, but let's imagine that you meet someone, discover an opportunity, the stars align and you're offered a steady job, why at the very point when the sand in the hourglass is speeding up, would you be keen enough on a brand, a company or a boss to give them eight hours (sometimes more) out of the twenty-four that life kindly allocates us each day?

Isn't it time for a new rhythm? So you can enjoy the company of the person you love most in the world: yourself. Take back what belongs to you and what's running away from you: time! Make it the Gordian knot of your freedom, the centre of what you do, the witness to the bitter-sweet imperfection of reality.

At this point, I can hear the comments: 'That's a nice idea, but the centre of what I do is bringing home the daily bacon, so stopping work is all well and good, but what am I going to do for $$$?'

Above all, it's about finding an idea that fits with the life we'd like to lead. An idea that suits us, that's achievable and will turn a reliable profit, even if it's only a modest one, in the short and medium term. Buying land to plant almond trees is a nice idea, but as it takes at least five to ten years to see even a hint of a crop, it's a bit late in the day, given that we're already in our fifties, as you know. So leave the long-term plans to a younger patient.

You could grow something. Or rather go into permaculture, which is above all a lifestyle. Diversified production and clever marketing of a sexy ingredient (honey, saffron, kale, chia seeds . . .). Apply to work in a patisserie, as a saleswoman, in a museum or a bookshop. You could sign up for a philanthropic programme, help people, make yourself useful. How? Give, give, give, a little of your time, a little of yourself.

Organising your future life

Redefine your centres of interest, decide on a plan and try to make a success of it. But the problem is that too much time sends us into a panic and we constantly put off the tasks on our daily road map.

Reinventing a new professional life, in the age of the cult of youth and Uberisation, is not easy. So to ease our passage through the hairpin bend of change, we can direct our energy into an age-old attitude that's now become very fashionable: laziness. Sometimes theorised, rarely justified and often mocked, laziness isn't as shameful as it's made out to be, it's just a minor defect, a rebellion against freneticism, almost an *art de vivre*[*]. The current manifesto urges us not to try to pin any guilt on those who aspire to laziness. Especially if they go about their business discreetly, asking nothing from anyone, and all the more so if it's only a transitional period, which is often the case.

With its two little sisters, Slowing Down and Cutting Back, Laziness with a capital L becomes a delectable approach to life that mostly brings balance and well-being to those who practise it regularly. Highly recommended

---

[*] Translator's note: the very French concept of the 'art of living'.

for the heart and the mind, it wipes out stress, helps you to breathe and allows you to devote quality time to yourself and others.

Laziness gives you time to think, meditate and philosophise, which can become a full-time activity. We should reread Epicurus, Thoreau, Emerson, Lafargue . . . The current trend is for a return to the self and the simple life. So let's shift gear, and happily embrace this slower pace. But whilst I'm slowing down the tempo in this new life, I'll ensure that my head and its contents are constantly alert and on the look-out, waiting in ambush. At the first rustle of a branch, I aim, fire and hit my target . . . Like before. And perhaps even better than before!

'Darling, why don't you have a lie down, it'll pass,' says Le Doux, who's a little concerned after reading these lines, which he interprets as an existential crisis that needs to be nipped in the bud as soon as possible. 'We'll cancel our subscription to *Philosophie Magazine* and stop going to Charles Pépin's* lectures for a while, OK? We'll take a break from all that thinking.'

'WHAT? No more Charles Pépin lectures? Oh no, not that!'

---

* Translator's note: a popular philosopher who gives weekly lectures open to the public in Paris. Think open-necked shirt and shoulder-length hair rather than a stuffy academic.

How to fight procrastination

Ask me the question, and I'll tell you that I'll have a nice quiet think about it and get back to you tomorrow or the day after. Le Doux, who has a lot to teach me in many areas, including the art of procrastinating, asks me with a touch of irony: 'So, that bit about procrastination, how's it coming on?' Grrrr.

To help me put things off until tomorrow, I'm constantly inventing distractions and prolonging the moments when I do anything but what I'm supposed to.

For three weeks, I've been guiltily delighting in a case of writer's block. I procrastinate with a mixture of joy and shame. It's a curious attitude that flirts with laziness, puts you in the slow lane, and allows all kinds of powerful diversions to come to the front of the queue for attention.

The internet in general and social networks in particular are wonderful fields of expression where you'll find a compendium of distractions ranging between indifferent voyeurism and pointless curiosity.

Which is why, before beginning the first sentence, I succumbed to the temptation of a visit to the Amazon books section, before very quickly finding myself beset by all kinds of highly consumerist temptations (ASOS, Vestiaire Collective . . .) which encouraged me (in spite of myself) to undertake a comparative analysis of underwear, shoes, coats . . . all of it at bargain prices.

I try a cup of tea to boost my inspiration, and as it brews, take a call from a friend with nothing particular to say, but who spends a long time saying it. Then I have a poke around LinkedIn, where people are exchanging compliments to help them find work or clients, and spend a lot of time on Facebook, where people are busy 'liking' each other and sharing pictures of their toes with a tropical lagoon in the background, before taking a little detour on homeforexchange, where some bright sparks are trying to swap a three-room apartment out in Batignolles for a loft in Soho.

Still not a single line written.

Before I get caught up in the news, which has an uncanny ability to kidnap your time with its never-ending sources of information, I take a peek at Coursera to see what's new, then tell myself it's time for a bit of exercise. So I open up the timetable for my dance centre. If I run I can make it to a Modern Jazz class. I'll be finished at 8 p.m., still without having written a line.

At the end of the day, I'll check that I've notched up more steps than yesterday on my fitness tracking app, before reading TTSO* and giving some more thought to the fact that time obstinately refuses to give us more than twenty-four hours, around a third of which is entirely devoted to our Queen and King (-sized beds). (At this point, Le Doux starts to coo and fan out his tail.)

Money . . .

O genie of the lamp, if I can't have it myself, let me always have friends who have enough.

Money was invented to be spent. For your own pleasure, and to bring pleasure to those you love, for culture and for wellbeing. Both provident and profligate, be sure not to neglect the extravagant treats, but still keep a close eye on your accounts. At fifty, money should no longer be an issue, whether you have it or not. Either way, the fat lady has sung. All the more so as it's 2018 and we fifty-somethings were clever enough to be born at the right time to take advantage of the benefits of an era when money was easier to come by and property more affordable. A form of growth that won't be coming back anytime soon, they say.

Renting out your apartment occasionally, or just a

---

* Translator's note: a light-hearted daily email digest of the news.

room, is a fairly uncomplicated approach that has the triple advantage of increasing your income, letting you meet people from all over the world, and sparing you the hassle of having to move house. All good reasons to stay in an apartment that's been too big for you since the children moved out.

You can rent it out from time to time, but also exchange, because these days, holiday homes are other people's homes, whether you rent, share or swap.

My experience of apartment swapping

Our respective taxis crossed paths on the road to the airport and we laughed (I'm sure) about the absolutely identical notes we left on the dining room table next to the bottle of champagne: 'Welcome. Enjoy your stay.' For three months, an American couple slept in my bed while I was in theirs, in New York, on the 38th floor of a glass tower surrounded by buildings, which nevertheless offered a verdant glimpse of Central Park. I've been a fan of apartment swapping for many years now. It's something I'm extremely relaxed about and has allowed me to stay all over the world. It's better to be separated from your possessions and objects, to be reminded that they're inanimate and have no soul. Trust goes without saying, being both mutual and necessary. This social, international property swapping means I can have a whole host of second homes all around the world and the network of connections that goes with them. It's the new economy for tourism – social and nomadic – and as good young fifty-somethings, we have no problem adapting. Occasionally, when I hear someone say, 'I don't want people I don't know sleeping in my bed,' I point out that you don't have to be there at the time.

Cut down

Plan for a process of cutting down. Get rid of all your excess baggage. There's too much of everything. We have an urgent need to learn to get rid of the things that have lost their allure or are only alluring to dealers in second-hand luxury goods. Jewellery from an ex (sell it!), an old coat (ejected!), a Chanel number picked up at an exclusive sales event in 1994 (heave-ho), a chest of drawers (out it goes), a painting (hello, Gumtree) . . . There's no downside to getting rid of your old stuff. Sell. Swap. Recycle. Come up with new revenue streams: hire out your car, sub-let your house. Go green and save money. Car-share, recycle plastic and paper bags, opt for filtered water and a pretty carafe and never buy another multi-pack of mineral water.

If you liked overconsumption, you're going to love preaching the opposite approach; embrace your contradictions. Think about the lifestyles of our slightly older friends who were Maoists back in the 1970s. Hilarious. They all put their kids through private schools, and some of them, surprised by the easy money that rained down on them thanks to the post-war boom, now can't help thinking that those tax planning advisors charge some pretty outrageous fees.

Social life and etiquette

Is our capacity to see, observe and listen to other people still intact? When did we last meet someone we felt an instant connection with? When did we think to ourselves, as if it went without saying, 'I like this person, I'd like to know more,' as if it was self-evident? It either happens or it doesn't. Our relationships with other people are a moveable feast, the tectonic plate of friendship circles moves according to availability, contacts and partners.

Never forget to be curious about other people, the ones you haven't got to know yet.

What time for dinner? What shall I bring?

These two questions, which come just after 'OK for the 25th' and before 'see you tonight x' on the text message scale, are the sort of standard pieces of politeness we ought to do away with. We ask them in the full knowledge that we'll pay no attention to the expected answers: '8.30. Nothing.'

We'll do what we want anyway, because whatever happens, we'll arrive when we arrive and we'll bring what we like, depending of course on how much we're looking forward to the dinner and how fond we are of the host (and also the ratio of our means to our generosity).

There's a code to the arrival time: 7.30 says 'I'm coming straight from the office; I'm going to bed early; I'm an American.' 9.30 says 'I'm an artist; you live too far away; I had another thing to go to first.' So if you want to avoid an extended aperitif that means you've already had a skinful of peanuts by the time you sit down to eat, you're better off inviting people with the same professional and familial biorhythms. The average arrival time of around 8.45 is a happy medium for those with jobs and the rest.

So what to bring with you? At our age, it's rare for someone to reply, 'Bring a quiche,' unless it's some sort of practical joke. In the normal run of things, we've all still got friends who offer us a free hot meal, in tacit exchange for sharing our good humour, a few anecdotes and a bottle of something from the fridge.

Good humour is the minimum politeness demands, but it also depends on the other guests following suit. Downers are like the bad apple in the fruit bowl – they spread quickly. That's why we forget to invite depressives, even though they're the ones with the greatest need, but what can you do?

If you have made the mistake of being invited at the same time as someone fixated on their misfortunes who has no qualms about sharing them with the other guests, you urgently need to turn things around by transforming the rest of the party into a schizophrenic release. My recommendation as a woman who's seen a few: improvise something festive. Why not turn up the volume and dance, or perhaps opt for the latest craze on an evening out: each guest takes it in turn to tell everyone their most awkward situations or epic failures. Laughs and surprises are guaranteed.

Even the most talkative guest (who isn't always the most interesting) will still leave you some opportunities to come up with the odd anecdote. You always need one to hand, recent for preference, so as to avoid repeats or tired material. I envy the talent that some people have of ensuring everyone gets to do their fair share of talking. Personally, I find myself paralysed when a dinner table suddenly falls silent, and I'm infinitely grateful to the person who can restart the conversation.

Like anyone else, I have a few 'bad apples' in my address book, who've been there since the dawn of time, but I love them whatever their misfortunes or all-consuming neuroses and I make sure not to forget them, because you never know, the sun's shining for me right now, but one day (maybe never), if the wheel turns and the planets align into a slightly twisted Z shape, I know my old apples will be there for me.

How to cancel for a better offer

In these piranha-infested waters where solitary and socialised egos rub up against each other, where living in Paris in these tough times means that if you don't play to win at all costs you at least need to play your cards right, it is indispensable to know the elementary rules for survival in an acid environment and learn to use sleight of hand in the swamp.

It might seem a bit cynical, but frankly, can the person who's never cancelled a dinner with a desperate friend for a last-minute opportunity with a good-looking gentleman or a funky evening with some movers and shakers raise their hand or cast the first stone!

Well? I'm looking, I'm listening . . .

There you go. No one. I knew it!

Could it be the fault of urban life? Our obsessive individualism, our overblown egocentricity, or the 'me first' culture fed by an unavoidable connectivity that heightens all known forms of narcissism?

So how do you do it without getting found out?

'I passed out in the metro' demands an explanation.

'I'm really tired' is a little thin.

'I forgot I was supposed to go swimming' is clearly taking the piss.

'My aunt died' takes a bit of nerve.

'I've got a stomach bug' puts you in quarantine.

'I've been pick-pocketed, I've got to go to the police station' isn't bad, but needs explanations: Oh really, where was that? How did it happen?

Personally, having been brought up with old-fashioned values, I advocate a kind of compromise with the truth. Why not suggest another date: something along the lines of 'Instead of tomorrow, do you fancy meeting up the day after, because I've got a surprise for you?' Then you have twenty-four hours to come up with the surprise (concert, theatre, networking . . .). Because opportunities don't come that often, and desperate friends are here to stay.

The difficulty comes on New Year's Eve. Suggesting something better the next day could be difficult. But in this case, you have a free pass. The whole of the Paris party crowd is busy setting a new record for cynicism as they wait for a better plan, right up to the last minute. That's why you should NEVER try to hold a dinner-for-twelve-style New Year's Eve party. You'll end up losing your temper with your so-called friends, and be left with a turkey on your hands that you have to freeze in small portions and carry on eating until Easter.

Alcohol, our faithful friend

We're not born equal when it comes to alcohol. That's just the way it is. But where we are more or less equal is that at fifty, we can no longer drink the way we'd like to. Whether it's down to genetics, metabolism, our livers, climate change or the new-generation pesticides that give us those crippling headaches the next day . . .

Our ability to cope with drink decreases with age. Its effects grow over the years, and the behavioural tendencies of our youth are magnified. Those who tottered will stumble, those who became talkative under the influence won't even pause for breath, and those who became amorous will take their passion to valiant new levels.

My friend Edwige becomes very funny when she drinks. And because she knows it, she's been drinking more and more, for the greater good, for as long as I can remember. She starts quite early, planning to raise a first glass around 6 o'clock, putting her on an increasingly steep slope, before she begins her proper night out at around eleven. These are the two ends of the social candle that she's inexorably burning too often.

There comes a point when her funny behaviour undergoes a sort of genetic modification. Her laugh turns strange, staccato and thin, her words come unravelled, she loses the thread and tells stories that don't make sense and go on for ever. It's time! She doesn't stumble, which is something, but as one minor effect can hide another, under the influence of alcohol, her libido can suddenly flare up and if there happens to be a consenting red-blooded male to hand . . . Luckily, this isn't always the case. Very quickly, she exhausts herself, and her audience watches her sink into confusion, slightly disconcerted, with a perverse goodwill. The day after, she remembers nothing. But as she knows what she's like, she apologises to the lady of the house, without really knowing what for.

Priska gets jealous and slightly bitter when she drinks. She's a good-looking fifty-something, who in an increasingly distant past was a very beautiful woman. In contact with alcohol, she turns aggressive. Flames come out of her eyes and her teeth are ready to bite. At one point, she had it in for me when she'd had a bit to drink. I have to admit I was slightly flattered. I interpreted her drunken comments as compliments. But for a while, she's been quite nice to me. It's disconcerting. Either she's stopped drinking, or I've suddenly got older.

Cécile turns amorous and demonstrative when she drinks. One glass too many transforms her into a puppy who licks you all over. She hugs you, clasping you to her breasts, which is a little embarrassing, saying, 'I love you, my darling, you know I love you.' Her neurosis met its match in Laurent, who shares a similar relationship with alcohol. They have nothing in common besides this shared reaction to drink. So they're only in love when they're drunk. As long as they were drunk together and often, it was OK, but since one of them decided to stop drinking, their relationship has fizzled out.

As for me, once, a long time ago, I needed at least four glasses of wine to guarantee a migraine the next day. Today, two is enough to have me reaching for the Zomig, provided I take it in time. Otherwise, the union rate is three days in bed, eyes closed, with a bag of ice on my forehead.

I've always thought that migraines were saving me

from inevitable social alcoholism, but my abstinence cuts me off from an atmosphere that develops and heats up as the evening wears on. So I'm left there as a mute observer of a table of people talking faster and faster, laughing louder and louder about things that as far as I can see, are less and less funny. I'm struck dumb when I drink, it turns out my light. I think I'm funnier when I climb out of bed in the morning.

Think about that before you invite me to dinner.

Happily, Le Doux makes up for it. Thanks to his Polish roots, he can ingest litres of alcohol without any side-effects besides an exaggerated demonstration of his feelings. He's never drunk whatever the volume, never ill whatever the mixtures, and grows amorous when he drinks to my great delight.

Funny stories

There are those who tell them and those who listen.

At the end of a dinner, usually after a gap in the conversation and a good bottle, someone (usually a man) will pipe up with a good one (a story to tell, that is).

Funny stories are like peanuts, you can never stop at one, and so it goes on, till they're all gone. The laughter inspired by the storyteller often encourages the other males in the gathering to get theirs out (stories, that is). All for the benefit of us girls, who enjoy seeing them cheerfully crossing swords to see who's got the longest, and expending all their efforts solely for the virile objective of making us laugh.

Whilst funny stories always create a good atmosphere, I'm slightly petrified by three things. First, that it will drag on – because those who pick up the microphone are sure of themselves, the room's on their side, and they take advantage. In these cases, it's amusing to watch the story-teller's other half, whose attitude is a barometer of their relationship: a wife of twenty years starts clearing the table, thinking 'this one lasts six minutes, I've got time to load the dishwasher.' The woman who's been with him five years and also knows the joke is still good enough to smile from start to finish. As for the recent conquest, she's grinning from ear to ear and still laughing about it now!

My second fear is that the story will cross the line. You're never far from veering off-limits and the fact that the audience laughs about one slightly shocking story gives licence for the next one to go a little further. Cue awkwardness, forced laughter or disgrace. 'Would anyone like a herbal tea?' ventures the mistress of the house, hoping to create a diversion. Too late. Who knows another one? We start on the Belgians this time, then escalate, but you're never very far from putting your foot in it and offending the guy sitting next to you.

Finally, my last fear is the worst: I'm scared I won't get the joke.

But in that case, no one will know, because come what may, never fear, I'll laugh heartily at the right moment along with everyone else.

Do you still get an invite to a thirty-year-old's birthday?

If we disregard exceptions along the lines of scientific mysteries, hypnosis gone wrong, shamanic worship or misaligned constellations, there are things that NEVER happen to a woman in her fifties anymore, however young she is.

We should admit, for example, that we're no longer going to have a friend who's pregnant, go home with a stranger blind drunk at the end of an after party, leave our husband of thirty years (of marriage, not thirty years old), breast feed, make love three times a night, have a sneaky hamburger in the afternoon or be invited to a birthday party for someone under forty . . .

But in fact it is possible, and not long ago, we were invited to celebrate a thirty-fifth birthday.

Thirty-five! My goodness, it feels like yesterday, but clearly, it was a very long time ago. So who do we know who could be thirty-five, apart from nieces and second cousins? Obviously, the invitation was the result of an inter-generational relationship (i.e. a twenty-year age gap). She was the one with the birthday, not him (have you notice that no one mentions Brigitte Macron's birthday?), and they'd both invited their friends. Which means that half the crowd was thirty-five and the other half fifty-five. Everyone rubbed along together very happily in this 50:50 thirty/fifty mixture, and in the second half, we pulled our weight on the dance floor, shaking our joints to the big hits of the 1990s (Desireless, Philippe Lafontaine, Chagrin d'amour . . .) that the DJ was kind enough (or charitable enough) to prioritise.

A few observations from the event:

Thirty-somethings know the words of OUR songs by heart, almost better than we do. But why? It remains a great mystery, because we'll never know the words to rap hits by La Fouine or Maître Gims.

Stevie Wonder when the cake arrives is a thing of the past. Forget 'Happy Birthday to You', you come up with your own accompaniment. We quickly opened up Shazam to identify what the DJ had chosen for the moment when we all gathered round the queen of the night, and he really went for it. The music was so loud! Much louder than 'in my day' and rendering all communication impossible, apart from the hand by your ear with your three middle fingers folded down to say, 'we'll talk on the phone'. There was a dull ringing in my battered ears long after the festivities were over.

In twenty years, the way we dance has changed. A thirty-year-old keeps time with her right arm, an out-stretched index finger rising and falling in a robotic rhythm whilst the head and the hips move like they're on springs. Fifty-somethings operate differently. First of all, they're the only ones who dance to something from another century by the name of rock. And then, amongst the solo performers, there are those who gently nod their heads, and others (like me) who never got over *Fame* or the final audition in *Flashdance*, and let loose until something snaps (a heel or a tendon).

As the clock struck one, the mood took a sudden nose-dive. Where were our fifty-something accomplices on the dance floor?

'The old people have gone home to bed,' I said to Le Doux.

'Only the young ones are left,' he replied (the implica-tion being 'us'). In fact, I could see the fifty-somethings, clustered round the open bar, plucking up courage. They were doing sterling work with the vodka that the wait-resses poured generously into their water glasses. A final layer of alcohol after the champagne and the wine, before the final frenetic flurry on the dance floor whilst the young ones called it a night.

The next day, all the same, arrange for a massage, an aspirin, a coffee and a few days of abstinence, all washed down with detoxifying herbal teas, and then don't move for a week, unless you want to discover aches and pains there, there and there.

A dinner in Long Island

A few years ago, the family sold the company whose name has remained synonymous with a sparkling, fes-tive beverage, and since then, they've divided their time between several countries. They're likeable and blasé, egocentric and cultivated. They're spoiled children who know they don't deserve what they've got but act like it's all a foregone conclusion. They vote for the right and make no secret of it, think democracy has its limits, that lawyers go too far, and are fighting to have Napoleon III's ashes returned to France. They'd almost describe them-selves as royalists, invent some noble origins and inject themselves with blue blood. Don't hope for a question about you, your life or what you've done. It's just they don't care! Or maybe it's out of politeness. The rich have their rules, and if you want to be invited back, you need to be able to identify the taboo words and subjects: employment protection schemes, unions, stool tests, the fifteenth arrondissement, Victor Serge*, anywhere outside central Paris . . . Avoid asking, 'What do you do for a living?' You'll be forgiven for having the poor taste to ask, and the answer will lie somewhere between philanthropy and looking after their own fortunes. In short, they're deliciously decadent. In their mansion, a hybrid of Tara, Disneyland and J.R.'s house, you'll hear English, French and Spanish. Everyone's assumed to be trilingual. The guests enjoy the ubiquity of the discreet staff and the polite frivolity of the conversation. The master of the house has long, thinning hair and striped socks. His eyes are two horizontal slits beneath his high-arched eyebrows. He looks like the tiger in *The Jungle Book*, feigning sleep, but you wouldn't want to bet on it. His wife is a virtuoso cook, she's slim, slender and muscular. It looks like a full-time job. Their whole little world is likeable, obliging and untroubled, with the only apparent concerns being the choice of sun protection factor, sharing tips about

---

* Translator's note: the Russian revolutionary and opponent of Stalin who took refuge in Belgium and France.

the best suppliers and seeking out the most exclusive distractions.

Socialising, slowing down and not getting too hung up on social media

There are a thousand different ways to showcase our egos on the internet. Facebook and Twitter are the barometer of our emotions, and LinkedIn, where we go to build each other up, regularly sends its regards. All this effort we put into being liked, read, bought, hired or sold, in order to seduce or simply to exist.

Our social media stimulate this rise in narcissism that forces us to curate our image and remind all our friends and followers just how happy and lucky we are. Of course, those who claim to be often aren't, because as we know, spending your life posting on the internet is a little suspect.

In spite of my criticism, I still like looking at other people's pictures, choosing a pretty photo and a well-honed comment. An exercise that can be given a bit of a literary twist. So no, social media apps are not the devil, you just need to be sure to keep them at arm's length. The frenetic digital acceleration that means things instantly go out of fashion, the rush for 'likes', the genuine interest in other people's joy: we just need to think before we spend too much time on it.

Should you accept holiday invitations?

Spending your holidays as guests of rich friends is always cheaper than sharing a holiday cottage with poor ones. Of course, not everyone is lucky enough to know people who are wealthy and generous enough (one quality without the other is no use), but if you're likeable, funny and well brought-up, you might find yourself being asked: 'What are you doing this summer?' There's a long, wavering silence as you hold back your joy, and with sparkling eyes, shoot your husband a selfless look and say in a slightly detached tone: 'We haven't decided on anything yet.' Don't rush in, don't give any radical replies, leave the door ajar and wait for the details. To avoid any surprises, be sure to ask the right questions.

Will there be children there? If yes, what ages? Who's on the guest list?

After a short pause for thought, if the children are under fifteen and some sort of communal approach is planned, forget about it. You and your man will find somewhere else, anywhere else. You can resume social niceties on your return. But if you find out that the house has six bedrooms, all en suite, that the guests are interesting people with a compatible sense of humour, and the proposal includes a full-time domestic servant and a motorboat, then go for it!

But don't forget that there are rules to holiday squatting. You don't have any rights, but if you want to come back for a second year or keep on good terms, this very practical form of holiday-making involves a host of duties that it would be dangerous to avoid and prudent to perform.

Stand firm on the length of stay: never more than four days. I'll spare you the inelegant comparison I heard this summer about friends on holiday and fish in the fridge. But unless it's an invitation to somewhere inaccessible, you're better off sticking to this rule about time.

Remember a gift for Madame (book, perfume, plate, bag, knick-knacks . . .) and the obligation to maintain a sunny disposition throughout, be quick to smile (without making yourself look simple), attentive to your hosts' conversation, and set aside your radically provocative views (you know you have them, we all do). For example, avoid starting conversations about delicate issues: bullfighting, environmentalism, labour law or migrants . . . Opt for subjects that everyone can identify with: property, tourism, the latest issue of *Voici** or *Philosophie Magazine*, be sure to treat the suggestion of a game of backgammon as an excellent idea if it comes from your bountiful host, help out where necessary, remember to leave a tip for the cleaner when you leave, and send a thank you letter (by text, naturally).

Maybe one day, you will be the bountiful host.

---

* Translator's note: celebrity news and gossip magazine.

Go Girls!

If you're reading these lines, it's a good sign, or it should be, unless you've done what I sometimes do and started at the end.

So here we are at the end ('already' would be presumptuous). A book is quite an adventure!

The itinerary of its observations, the history of its development, the course of its meanderings, the fluctuating beliefs, the thoughts laid bare, and all the underlying work required by a desire to have fun with everything from words to ideas and situations.

What an adventure, and what a pleasure to challenge your motivation and appeal to your memory, to doubt, retain, reject, reclaim, hone, abandon, select, remove, begin again, go back and finally finish.

The word END is terrifying, it makes me want to turn around and go back.

As you read these pages, by way of a conclusion, I'd like to lift your spirits one more time and end with a final spritz of impertinent optimism. I'd also like to give you a few key bits of advice to help you savour this radiant decade a little more.

Put the bad times in your personal history through the sieve of memory and throw away the filter, only retaining the neutral information and constructive or pleasant experiences. Don't bother yourself over past difficulties and refresh your personal page each day so that you're never weighed down by things that you dwell upon, gloat over or regret.

I'm not going to preach to you about living in the present moment. There are enough personal development books to tell you how important it is to make *Carpe Diem* our motto, blah, blah, blah. But beyond observing the joys of everyday life, at fifty you'll also need to be able to dissolve your own sadness, practise forgetting, deal with your grey areas and take care of your melancholy, shaking it up sometimes, but always loving it. Feed on your solitude to help you regenerate. Venerate otherness, keep your eyes and your mind wide open. Take pleasure in active and unique hedonism. This is all that we learn over the course of this decade.

The conclusion to these thoughts is that everyone fills their baggage with what they decide to carry with them. Joy, good humour and kindness don't take up much room, unlike indignation, anger, complaints or bitterness . . .

To all women of fifty and over, and to the rest as well, I'd like to say that life begins again all the time, and can begin again at any time. You can encounter love in your fifties without warning, unexpectedly, like a happy accident, as they say of a child who wasn't entirely planned. One day, you inadvertently find yourself at the highest point of a marvellous landscape, under a blue sky in the pure air, defying your sense of vertigo, weighing up the fragility of these moments and holding your love tight for fear it might dissolve. You close your eyes, frightened that a stone could seize up the mechanism and threaten to bring the edifice tumbling down.

Sometimes, when I'm lost in my bad dreams, I'm on the edge of the chasm, my arm lets go, the rope snaps and I wobble. I find myself begging the gods, telling them how much I want to stay at the top, alive, loving, loved, magnetised, aware of each moment.

I want to keep this love-fuelled amazement, this desire for life, this infinite exaltation. I want:

To stay in the air,

Never to come back down,

To know only the absolute version of this love, sub-lime at the summit,

Lasting,

Strong,

Incarnate,

Knowing that one day, if the colours were to fade,

If the music were to turn discordant,

If our kisses and hearts were to dry up,

If we no longer had this slight anxiety about losing one another, and if one of us wanted to leave and live another life . . .

Let's hope we would have enough love for the other not to stand in the way.

And enough for ourselves not to try.

In any case, it will be nothing to do with age.

Because the end is never the end.

These days, the internet makes it easier to meet people and, more than ever before, we have reasons to be loved for what we are, without the absurd or outdated judge-ments of the old days. Women in their fifties are no longer what they were. We're living in a world where age no longer means the same thing, happy that the old prejudices are no more, and women in our society are no longer seen as creatures of reproduction, of servi-tude, of passing satisfaction or trophies, valued above all for the fleeting quality of youth. We have an amazing opportunity to fulfil ourselves, to express ourselves, to be heard, and to give as much as we receive. By overturning the rules of the old world, our generation has brought this decade to life.

So amidst the acceleration of what seems to be the final straight of our lives, let's voraciously make the most of everything, triumph over the remnants of the past, shake the glass globe and watch in amusement as the snow falls.

A hundred years ago, fifty per cent of us would already have been dead, and fifty years ago, 100 per cent of us would already have been old women, whereas today, with the help of apps, cosmetics, science, the promise of immortality, feminism, male–female equality, smart scales, food supplements and good luck, which is sure to return even if it's lacking at the moment, we are all, and will be for many years to come, young fifty-somethings.

Acknowledgements

Warm and sincere thanks to Karina Hocine-Bellanger (angel), for putting her faith in me;

Jeanne Morosoff, (up and coming angel), for her editorial support, which was always pertinent, and always obliging;

Michel Munz for his wise advice at each stage of the writing process, for his devastating humour and our life full of love.

Thank you to Virginie Luc, Fabienne Azire, and Florence Le Lous for reading my work and encouraging me.

Thank you to my dear friends, most of them young fifty-somethings, my heroines, my sources of inspiration, from whom I allowed myself to steal some anecdotes. Despite the use of assumed names, they'll recognise themselves. Alexandra, Anne, Catherine, Cosy, Constance, Florence, Marie, Marie-Francoise, Nat, Nice, Papesse and Virginie.

The same goes for the menfolk; thank you to Antoine, Bertrand, Laurent, Fabrice, François and Jean-Christophe. There are others, but will they recognise themselves?

Thank you to the subscribers to my blog Happy-Quinqua (www.happyquinqua.com) for their loyalty.

And loving thoughts, always, to my dear children Timotée and Danaé. I'm so proud of you.